M

Cuisines *of the* Alps

The Hippocrene Cookbook Library

Afghan Food & Cookery
African Cooking, Best of Regional
Albanian Cooking, Best of
Alps, Cuisines of The
Aprovecho: A Mexican-American Border
  Cookbook
Argentina Cooks!, Exp. Ed.
Austrian Cuisine, Best of, Exp. Ed.
Belgian Cookbook, A
Bolivian Kitchen, My Mother's
Brazilian Cookery, The Art of
Bulgarian Cooking, Traditional
Burma, Flavors of
Cajun Women, Cooking With
Calabria, Cucina di
Caucasus Mountains, Cuisines of the
Chile, Tasting
Colombian, Secrets of Cooking
Croatian Cooking, Best of, Exp. Ed.
Czech Cooking, Best of, Exp. Ed.
Danube, All Along The, Exp. Ed.
Dutch Cooking, Art of, Exp. Ed.
Egyptian Cooking
Eritrea, Taste of
Filipino Food, Fine
Finnish Cooking, Best of
French Caribbean Cuisine
French Fashion, Cooking in the
  (Bilingual)
Germany, Spoonfuls of
Greek Cuisine, The Best of, Exp. Ed.
Gypsy Feast
Haiti, Taste of
Havana Cookbook, Old (Bilingual)
Hungarian Cookbook
Hungarian Cooking, Art of, Rev. Ed.
Icelandic Food & Cookery
India, Flavorful
Indian Spice Kitchen
International Dictionary of
  Gastronomy
Irish-Style, Feasting Galore
Italian Cuisine, Treasury of (Bilingual)
Japanese Home Cooking
Korean Cuisine, Best of

Laotian Cooking, Simple
Latvia, Taste of
Lithuanian Cooking, Art of
Macau, Taste of
Mayan Cooking
Middle Eastern Kitchen, The
Mongolian Cooking, Imperial
New Hampshire: From Farm to Kitchen
Norway, Tastes and Tales of
Persian Cooking, Art of
Poland's Gourmet Cuisine
Polish Cooking, Best of, Exp. Ed.
Polish Country Kitchen Cookbook
Polish Cuisine, Treasury of (Bilingual)
Polish Heritage Cookery, Ill. Ed.
Polish Traditions, Old
Portuguese Encounters, Cuisines of
Pyrenees, Tastes of
Quebec, Taste of
Rhine, All Along The
Romania, Taste of, Exp. Ed.
Russian Cooking, Best of, Exp. Ed.
Scandinavian Cooking, Best of
Scotland, Traditional Food From
Scottish-Irish Pub and Hearth
  Cookbook
Sephardic Israeli Cuisine
Sicilian Feasts
Slovak Cooking, Best of
Smorgasbord Cooking, Best of
South African Cookery, Traditional
South American Cookery, Art of
South Indian Cooking, Healthy
Spanish Family Cookbook, Rev. Ed.
Sri Lanka, Exotic Tastes of
Swedish, Kitchen
Swiss Cookbook, The
Syria, Taste of
Taiwanese Cuisine, Best of
Thai Cuisine, Best of, Regional
Turkish Cuisine, Taste of
Ukrainian Cuisine, Best of, Exp. Ed.
Uzbek Cooking, Art of
Warsaw Cookbook, Old

Cuisines *of the* Alps

Recipes, Drinks, and Lore from France, Switzerland, Liechtenstein, Italy, Germany, Austria, and Slovenia

Kay Shaw Nelson

HIPPOCRENE BOOKS, INC.
NEW YORK, NY

To Rae and Karl who share my fondness for Alpine travel and food.

Book and jacket design by Acme Klong Design, Inc.

For more information, address;
HIPPOCRENE BOOKS, INC.
171 Madison Avenue
New York, NY 10016

ISBN 0-7818-1058-2
Cataloging-in-Publication Data available from the Library of Congress.
Printed in the United States of America.

Table of Contents

Acknowledgments

For this book I am especially grateful to the publisher, George Blagowidow, and my editors, Anne McBride and Rebecca W. Cole, of Hippocrene Books. As always, I wish to thank my daughter, Rae, for her continual support and editorial assistance while writing the book.

Over the years, many friends and acquaintances have helped considerably in my quest to produce an Alpine guide that is part history book, part travelogue, and part cookbook. I thank them all, especially those I knew when I lived in Germany. These include my husband, Wayne Nelson, Elizabeth Richards, Nellie Spiegler, Mary and Greg Hutchison, and Catherine and Matt Matthews. Before and after that period, many friendly people and culinary experts in Alpine countries shared their special knowledge of folklore, culinary traditions, and recipes with generosity. Some even spent hours with me in markets, kitchens, and provided hospitality through friendly conversations, the enjoyment of libations, and dining on fine fare.

I also wish to thank the Austrian and Swiss Tourist Boards and the Liechtenstein National Tourist Office for their valuable information.

Preface

It was a marvelous sunny autumn day and I was traveling with my husband from Milan, Italy, through Switzerland en route to northeastern France. Even with the anticipation of finally seeing the Alps, the most dramatic mountains in the world, it was difficult to express the exultation of my experience. At the first sight I was transfixed. Call them what you wish, magical, romantic, awesome, there is an enchantment about the majestic snow-capped peaks that beckons visitors year after year. Enthusiastic travelers come to France, Switzerland, Liechtenstein, Italy, Germany, Austria, and Slovenia to enjoy spectacular scenery, health resorts and spas, summer and winter sports, historical, and cultural attractions, colorful folklore, hospitable people, and diverse culinary specialties.

After driving from Italy through the historic Simplon Pass we arrived in the incomparable canton of Valais, a picture-postcard land embracing the Rhone River valley, high Alpine settlements, magnificent orchards, flourishing vineyards, and formidable landscapes. We were soon enchanted by the stunning views of fabled mountains, thinking about the role they had long played in poetry and literature as well as mountaineering. Awestruck, we drove along winding roads through deep gorges and past green pastures to our first destination, the small town of Brig, known for centuries as a trading center with Italy and now an important rail and road junction joining four cantons. Its outstanding attraction is the massive baroque Stockalper Castle topped with three gilded onion domes, built in 1624 by a wealthy merchant, Kaspar Stockalper, called the uncrowned king of Valais.

We were in Brig, however, to enjoy my first Alpine meal and to explore the indigenous cooking. Many famous cooks have come from Valais and in most Swiss cities there are Valaisan restaurants serving specialties of the region that has long been famous for wine, chocolate, outstanding cheeses, and the freshest fruits and vegetables. The restaurant's rustic atmosphere was just perfect for enjoying *raclette*, originally from Valais and known all over Switzerland as a traditional country cheese dish that promotes conviviality, sparked by a lively interest in its preparation, service, and consumption. We also tasted the superlative air-dried beef made by marinating a piece of meat in herbs, pressed between planks, and then dried in the open air. Shaved into thin slices and virtually fat free, it is tender and flavorful.

I had no way of knowing that over the years, while living in Germany and traveling extensively in Europe, my family and I would enjoy a wealth of adventures and dining experiences not only in Switzerland but in the other Alpine countries as well. This is a rewarding area for exploration with the mountains forming a magical backdrop, sort of a key to the charm of any activity. The thrill of attending summer camp in the Swiss Alps, learning to ski in the Bavarian Alps, living on a farm in the Austrian Tirol, traveling with fellow students in northern Italy's historic cities, and exploring restaurants along France's Route Napoleon are experiences my daughter Rae will never forget. Wherever she happened to be, dining became a meaningful event, a time to learn about new foods and libations.

I discovered that while the daily Alpine fare is often hearty and wholesome, quite fitting for the cool climate, outdoor sports, and other vigorous activities, the regional specialties are surprisingly diverse. With friends from various nations I learned to cook many of the down-to-earth specialties using local ingredients. In my travels I dined in typical Alpine restaurants, cafés, and inns and celebrated at lively festivals, with colorful traditions and exuberance featuring the region's beloved foods, drinks, and music.

The cookery of the Alpine countries, a historically complex area comprising seven nations, is as fascinating to explore as it is to savor. This collection of distinguished cuisines contains a wealth of culinary treasures carefully evolved over the centuries by creative cooks. Indeed, the kitchens of these countries have produced cherished delicacies as well as flavorful hearty dishes that have an enduring appeal.

National and regional culinary traditions are highly respected and are taught to succeeding generations. Despite variations in soil, climate, and terrain, the productive areas have long been blessed by nature. Grazing lands are ample, and forests are rich with game. Rivers and lakes yield a plentiful supply of fish and seafood.

Still other factors have greatly affected the regional cuisine. The complicated culinary heritage is interwoven with the history of invasion and conquest, the influence of religious affiliation, and the effects of political and social orientation or allegiance, dictated by circumstances or by royal decree.

In any event, the cookery of the Alpine regions provides ample evidence that the people, whatever their regional or cultural differences, share a fondness for fine food. It is a tribute to them that, despite the rigors of a checkered history and the effects of political grouping and regrouping, the cuisines of the various countries retain distinct national and, in some cases, regional characteristics.

The charming late-nineteenth-century resort town of Chamonix, France, lies in a deep valley in the shadow of Mont Blanc, an area that has long lured dedicated Alpinists to its scenic location and sport attractions. Here I dined in cafés and at elegant restaurants where menus offer a prized selection of fine fare such as the rare tender fish, *ombre chevalier* and an exquisite warm raspberry soufflé. It was in historic Berchtesgaden, high in the Bavarian Alps that I discovered that according to tradition, *weisswurst*, a pale sausage of veal and bacon mixed with lemon and parsley, should be eaten before noon.

One of my most memorable meals was at the Schneefernerhaus, the highest hotel in Germany. It sits atop the Zugspitze, and is accessed by ascending the steep mountain in a cog train, switching to a cable car for the last stretch. In the handsome dining room with picture windows and terraces overlooking the mountains and ski slopes with a spectacular view of the German and Austrian countryside, I dined on a hearty nourishing soup called *eintopf*, made with lentils and sliced sausages. *Eintopf* creations, I learned, are enjoyed at family tables and amid the convivial *gemutlichkeit* atmosphere of a country inn or tavern.

I also have fond memories of meals enjoyed after visiting the wonderfully spectacular Bavarian castles, notably Linderhof, surrounded by fountains and sculpture gardens; Neuschwanstein, with fantasy turrets and picturesque Alpine setting; and the enormous yellow Hohenschwangau, all built by "mad" King Ludwig II. On the vine-covered terrace of one hostelry, the specialty of the house, called "Song without Words," a colorful display of foods, from appetizers to entrees was served on a large wooden platter. Elsewhere, I dined on *speiss*, a local specialty comprised of grilled pork, veal, and beef, interlarded on skewers with thin pieces of bacon and onion, in a rich wine sauce.

Austria's Tirol province, stretching from the Arlberg in the west to Salzburg in the east, the country's most popular tourist region, is noted for its breathtaking scenery, baroque churches, and picturesque villages. One of the most beautiful towns, particularly well known to international skiers, is Obergurgl, a tranquil village set in the spectacular grandeur of the craggy Oetztal Alps rising to 6,332 feet. The village is reached by a road closely following the Inn River, through deep forests and magnificent scenery. It's where deep snow lies late into spring and skiing is a supreme pleasure for veterans and beginners.

The town is popular as a family resort and I had the pleasure to vacation there with my daughter, her friends, and their parents. While they skied, I walked and explored the cookery of Tirol. We dined on hearty vegetable soups, meat dishes garnished with crisp onions and fried bacon, schnitzels, cheese-filled fritters, bread dumplings, and enticing rich pastries, such as great strudels and tortes.

Although the Alpine countries have been known for centuries for their summer and winter sports, they also provide marvelous opportunities for great dining. A love of good living has long been important and the people everywhere appreciate gastronomic delights.

This book contains a wide range of regional recipes with notes on native foods, and dining customs, offering an opportunity to experience some of the best culinary accomplishments of the Alpine countries. I hope that this book will enhance your knowledge of the region's cookery, add variety and interest to your menu, and brighten the dining experiences of everyone who sits at your table.

Introduction

A majestic mountain system in south-central Europe, the Alps form an approximately 750-mile arc from the Gulf of Genoa in the Mediterranean Sea to Albania in the southwest with dozens of peaks taller than 10,000 feet. They are divided into the Western Alps (southeastern France and northwestern Italy), the Central Alps (north-central Italy, southern Switzerland, and Liechtenstein), and the Eastern Alps (parts of Germany, Austria, and Slovenia), each of which contains several separate ranges including the Julian Alps.

The youngest of the world's great ranges, the Alps are fold mountains, or mountains formed from the folding of the earth's crust. They began to rise millions of years ago, when the African plate pushed smaller mountains against the Eurasian plate. Although characterized by high peaks and nearly vertical slopes, the landscape of the mountains in limestone regions of France and Italy is dominated by huge cliffs and canyons. Elevations average from 6,000 to 8,000 feet and among the hundreds of peaks over 10,000 feet, the highest is Mont Blanc in France at 15,781 feet.

There are a number of great Alpine crossings, famous for historical reasons and as roads or tunnels. The St. Gotthard, San Bernardino, and Grand St. Bernard road tunnels are the most convenient year-round connections between the north and south side of the Alps. There are also several pass roads that are open all year.

While the name Alps is often said to come from *alpes*, the Latin word for mountains, it is more widely believed to derive from the Celtic *alb*, or white, as the tops are perpetually covered with snow. According to another explanation, in Alpine regions the word *alp* has long denoted a high pasture, above the tree line and below the snow line, where the early herdsmen tended their flocks and herds with the peaks towering above them.

The Alpine relief, greatly influenced by glacial erosions, created considerable differences in the height of the mountain summits and valleys. Forming a divide between the Atlantic Ocean, Mediterranean Sea, and Black Sea, the Alps are the source of many European rivers, such as the Rhone, Rhine, Po, and numerous tributaries of the Danube. Because of their arc-like shape, the Alps separate the marine West Coast climates of Europe from the Mediterranean areas of France, Italy, and the Yugoslav region.

Because the Alps are tremendously high, once a wilderness of fear and superstition where it was believed dragons and ghosts inhabited the realms of ice and snow, it took centuries for scientists and mountaineers to explore the mysterious summits. Memories of the dramatic march of Hannibal, the Carthaginian general, traveling with a mixed force of soldiers and North African elephants across southern France and over the Alps, and terrifying pictures of the dangerous mountain tribes, enhanced the fears.

The father of European mountaineering was the great Swiss naturalist Horace Benedtict de Saussuer who, in 1787, climbed Mont Blanc. His experiences inspired other climbers and, between 1854 and 1865, the golden age of mountain climbing, most of the Alpine peaks were scaled. The first Alpine Club was founded in London in 1857.

English romantic poets and writers, especially Lord Byron and Percy Shelley found inspiration in Alpine views. "I never knew, I never imagined, what mountains were before," Shelley wrote about his first visit to France's Chamonix. Ever since Thomas Cook began conducting tours to Switzerland in 1863, tourists, as well as writers, artists, and musicians have derived inspiration and pleasure in coming to the summer and winter playgrounds of the Alps for many reasons, including great dining.

The French Alps

A majestic barrier of mountains, the French Alps, rises along the southeastern border of France, soaring to their climax in Europe's highest peak, Mont Blanc, which Lord Byron called the "Monarch of Mountains." Its chief divisions, from north to south, are the Mont Blanc region; the Savoie (Savoy), lying along the Italian border; the Dauphine, of which Grenoble is the capital; the Hautes Alpes, centered around Briancon; and the Maritime Alps (Basses Alpes), extending down to the Cote d'Azur on the Mediterranean.

This is one of the most spectacular regions in Europe with many points of interest: castles, museums, picturesque villages and resorts, lofty mountain peaks, glaciers, gorges, and waterfalls. There are also the engineering achievements of the famous, panoramic 287-mile Route Napoleon, and the 416-mile *Route des Grandes Alpes* from Nice to Evian-les-Bains. Among the notable places is Chamonix, the oldest and largest French winter sports resort and in summer a center for mountain climbers, which lies in a deep valley surrounded by mountains that are among the highest in the entire Alpine chain. Others are Aix-Les-Bains, Annecy, Megeve, and the curious Mont Aiguille (Needle Rock), 6,662-feet high, first scaled in 1492, one of the earliest recorded ascents in mountaineering history.

Among the culinary specialties of the French Alps are toothsome pâtés; hearty soups; gratins; potato dishes (*pommes de terre dauphinoise* and *farcon*); cheese and eggs (*omelette a la savoyarde*); poultry and game (*poularde de Bresse*); mushrooms and truffles; fish (trout, salmon, crayfish); mountain hams; desserts and confections (nut and fruit pastries). The region is noted especially for its cheeses such as Reblochon, Beaufort, and Vacherin, and boasts several fine wines; a famous liqueur, Chartreuse; and a number of distilled drinks, as well as mineral waters.

The Swiss Alps

Switzerland, a beautiful and inviting landlocked mountainous nation situated in the south of central Europe, is a stunning Alpine nation. The Alps occupy the central and southern regions and make up sixty percent of the country, roughly a fifth of the total range. In the Bernese Alps, the main ridge of the Central Alps, are such towering peaks as the Finsteraarhorn (14,022 feet), the Aletschhorn (13,763), and the incomparable Jungfrau (13,642), acclaimed as one of the most beautiful summits in the world.

Although the average height of the mountains in the southern Alps is 5,600 feet, some one hundred peaks reach 13,000 feet or more. The highest point is Dufour Peak, Dufourspitze, of Monte Rosa at 15,203 feet, although Matterhorn at 14,692 feet is better known. The most photographed of mountains, famous for its knifelike ridges and overhanging precipices, Matterhorn was once considered a great challenge to mountain climbers, and was first ascended in 1865 by a British team.

Extending along the upper Rhone Valley from Lake Geneva, the canton of Valais, an area of great natural beauty and dramatic Alpine scenery, is rich in history, folklore, art treasures, and natural wonders, including the country's highest mountains. It offers great opportunities for mountaineering in summer and skiing in winter at such famous resorts as Zermatt, one of the great tourist towns at the foot of Matterhorn. Others are Verbier, scenically situated on a natural terrace; and Saas-Fee, called a "Pearl of the Alps," encircled by fiercely glaciated 13,000-foot peaks, and known for its spas and winter sports.

Often called the country's kitchen garden and orchard, Valais has marvelous fruits and vegetables, and is also known for its lamb and cheese dishes as well as wine production, especially the sparkling white Fendant and ruby red Dôle.

The Bernese Oberland, a magnificent area comprised of lovely lakes, valleys, and the Bernese Alps in the southern canton of Bern, stretching from Gstaad in the west to the Sustern Pass in the east, has numerous spectacular attractions. Especially well known are Interlaken, situated as the name implies "between the lakes" of Thun and Brienz; the Jungfrau region; and Grindelwald, a famous resort. In many places the massifs, part of which are glaciated, rise above 13,124 feet.

One of Europe's most important watersheds, the St. Gotthard massif in central Switzerland is the source of many lakes and rivers, notably the Rhine and Rhone. For many centuries the massif was an obstacle to travel through the Alps, but construction of the St. Gotthard railway, and later the tunnel (the longest in the world) opened up this shortest route from north to south for modern travel. A series of high passes in the south provide overland access to Italy.

The canton of Grisons, also called Graubünden, known for its concentration of high Alpine peaks, beautiful lakes, and deep valleys, has some of the best known fashionable winter sports centers including Davos, Klosters, and St. Moritz, a 6,000-foot-high celebrated resort. A relatively unspoiled region of many contrasts, it has marvelous quaint villages and superb regional cooking.

Switzerland's cuisine has been extensively influenced by its three neighbors, France, Italy, and Germany but there also are great indigenous Swiss dishes. Cheeses form an important part of the diet and are used to make many famous specialties such as croquettes, soup, fondue and raclette. Others are *muesli*, bread and cheese soup, onion soup, dumplings, *rösti* (crisp, fried shredded potatoes), a variety of sausages, *Berner Platte* (pork and sauerkraut), salmon and trout dishes, veal in cream sauce, game dishes, fruit tarts, honey cakes, butter cookies, chocolate fondue, and hot chocolate. The country has notable wines and a number of fruit brandies.

The principality of Liechtenstein, a small charming independent nation situated between Austria and Switzerland along the eastern bank of the Rhine River and nestled in the Alps, is noted for its spectacular scenery with quaint villages, orchards, vineyards, and luxurious meadows. Covering only 62 miles, its way of life is a page from yesteryear, a great place for travelers, sports enthusiasts, and gourmets. One of its three distinct geographical areas is the edge of the Tirolean Alps in the southeast that has towering ranges of 7,000-foot peaks.

Nestled amid the mountains is the village of Malhun, the country's ski resort that has stunning Alpine vistas, breathtaking mountain hikes, and six hotels, each with a restaurant serving the country's appealing regional fare.

Among the Principality's national dishes are: *sauekas*, a piquant local cheese; hearty vegetable-meat soups; *hafalaab*, a one-dish meal made of wheat flour and cornmeal dumplings, simmered with smoked bacon or ham in broth; schnitzels; smoked pork and sauerkraut stews; venison; as well as cheese, meat, and vegetable fondues. Good desserts range from fruit-filled pancakes to rich pastries and cakes.

The Italian Alps

A spectacular mountain Alpine range lying in the northernmost part of Italy, not far from the Austrian border, is called the Dolomites, once described as "the most beautiful sculpture in the world." A remote region known for its rugged and austere beauty, the mountains, stretching from Trentino-Alto Adige into Veneto, were named for an eighteenth-century French geologist, Deodat de Dolomieu. The highest point is the Marmolada (10,964 feet), and the Drei Zinnen (Three Pinnacles) is rated as the most extraordinary limestone monolith in the Alps.

Totally unlike the Swiss Alps in silhouette, the Dolomites are a year-round mountain playground offering awe-inspiring scenery and great opportunities for the traveler, sportsman, and gourmet. Among the notable resorts and towns are Bolzano, a lively mountain city; the world famous ski-resort, Cortina d'Ampezzo, site of the 1956 winter Olympics; Trento, the historic capital of Trentino at the foot of Monte Bondone; and Verona, a city of great provincial charm. The impressive Parco dello Stelvio is the largest national park in the Alps, encompassing 40 lakes and the Alpine massif of Ortles-Cevedale that has a tenth of its terrain covered by glaciers.

While located in Italy, Trentino-Alto Adige's history is Austrian. Thus Austrian-Hungarian culinary influences are important, as are those from Germany. Typical wholesome dishes include: hearty pasta soups, minestrone, polenta, fish (trout, pike and golden perch), smoked meats, roast venison and rabbit, dumplings, noodles, a variety of sausages, sauerkraut, chicken-filled ravioli, mushroom risotto, gnocchi, *strangolapreti* (potatoes, bread or spinach dumplings), nut and fruit pastries, *erdbeertorte* (strawberry cake), and fruit preserves. The region produces superb cheeses such as Gorgonzola, Taleggio, and Grana Padona, wines, beer, and mineral waters.

The Austrian Alps

Austria, a small landlocked, pear-shaped nation, bordering seven other countries in the heart of Europe, is known for its spectacular mountains and lakes, chalet villages, traditional festivals, and high-spirited people. Two-thirds of the country is classified as mountainous with the Alps a dominating feature.

Three ranges, west to east, are the Northern Limestone Alps, on the border with Germany; the Central Alps, a longitudinal range with Austria's highest peak, the Grosslockner at over 12,461 feet; and the Southern Alps including the important Karavanken range, forming a natural barrier along the border with Italy and Slovenia.

The Tirol or Tyrol, Austria's famed mountain province and the most popular tourist region, stretches from the Arlberg in the west to the borders of Salzburg in the east, and south to the Brenner Pass. The province is known for its precipitous peaks, baroque castles, churches, and friendly people, and has notable medieval towns. Among them are Innsbruck, the capital in the Inn River Valley; Kitzbühel, famed as a winter sports center with picturesque gabled houses; Seefeld, a popular year-round resort; and Obergurgl, a 6,332-foot tranquil village in the craggy Oetztal Alps.

The Salzkammergut region, a delightful summer and winter playground of lakes, streams, and mountains with some of the most beautiful Alpine scenery in Europe, also has notable spa towns such as Bad Ischl with views of Mt. Katrin.

Among Austria's culinary specialties are Liptauer cheese, *Gerstlsuppe* (a barley soup), potato-cheese fritters, *wursts* (sausages), *Gebackene Schinkenfleckerl* (a ham-noodle soufflé), *Schlutzkrapfen* (spinach-cheese ravioli), *Tiroler grostl* (a meat-potato hash), goulash served with polenta, *Kirchtagskrapfen* (fruit-filled fritters), strudels, pancakes, cakes, and farmhouse cheeses. Austria is known for its interesting variety of wines, primarily white, as well as beer and distilled spirits.

The Bavarian Alps

In the extreme south of Bavaria, the largest of Germany's federated states, are the Bavarian Alps, extending east-northeast for 70 miles along the German-Austrian border and offering a marvelous vista of attractions. Consisting of heavily forested elevations over 5,000 feet, behind which rise steep ridges and high plateaus, they reach their highest peak in the 9,718 foot-Zugspitze of the Wetterstein Range, noted for its scenic beauty and for winter skiing and summer climbing activities. The mountains are crossed at the Scharnitz Pass (3,133 feet) by road and railway and at Aachen Pass (3,087 feet) by road.

Bavaria's most famous resort, Garmisch-Partenkirchen, a notable winter sports center and health resort, has hundreds of accommodations and facilities. When the Olympic Games were held here in 1936, the two small towns of Garmish and Partenkirchen were merged to form a single community. Lying on comparatively flat ground, the town is surrounded by mountains: the Wank to the east at 5,840 feet; the Kreuzeck to the south at 5,240 feet; and to the southwest, on the Austrian border, Germany's highest mountain, the majestic Zugspitze, reached either by cog railway or cable car.

Berchtesgaden, at the foot of the legendary Mount Watzmann, Germany's second highest mountain (8,901 feet) surrounded by majestic mountains, is a historical town boasting spa and sports facilities, a royal palace, and nearby salt mine. Today it is associated primarily with the name of Adolph Hitler who built his famed "Eagle's Nest" on the Obersalzberg, one of several high peaks near the Austrian border.

South of Berchtesgaden and deep in the national park, is the crystal clear five-mile-long Lake Konigsee, "King's Lake," where steep banks provide the most romantic scenery of Upper Bavaria, with Mount Watzmann towering above.

The German Alpine Road, running east from Berchtesgaden to Lindau on Lake Constance, is one of the most panoramic routes in the Alps. It features innumerable castles and palaces, marvelous lakes, picturesque villages and towns, as well as art treasures from many epochs.

Eating and drinking are important to the convivial Bavarian way of life celebrated in Gemütlichkeit, the spirit of warmth and fellowship. Traditional dishes include those made with meat, especially pork and veal, such as *Schweinebraten* and *Weisswurst* (spiced veal and pork sausages), sauerbraten, a variety of dumplings (knödel), noodles, fresh mushrooms in cream sauce, *Reiberdatschi* (baked grated potatoes served with applesauce), sauerkraut, sweet fruit dumplings, spice cakes, and pancakes.

Bavaria is famous for beer that comes in seasonal variations such as *Bockbier* (strong winter beer) and *Marzenbier*, popular at Munich's great autumn festival, the Octoberfest, and for summer, *Weissbier*. Enzian is a liqueur made from the root of the yellow gentian.

Slovenia's Julian Alps

Wedged between Austria and Croatia, and bordered by Hungary and Italy, the Republic of Slovenia, established in 1991, is a small prosperous country with a distinct centuries-old cultural heritage. It is known for its dramatic castles, lakes, friendly people, and majestic mountains, the vertiginous Julian Alps, culminating in the northwest. A range of the Eastern Alps, they extend southeastward from the Carnic Alps and the town of Tarvisio, a mountain resort in northeastern Italy, to near the capital city of Ljublijana (pronounced Loo-bee-ahn-ah). Composed primarily of limestone, the mountains are bounded by the Fella River and the Pass of Comporosso in the northwest, and by the Sava River in the north and east. They rise to the three-headed Mount Triglav at 9,396 feet, the highest point in Slovenia.

Forming part of the divide between the watersheds of the Adriatic and Black Seas, the mountains are separated into two sections by the Predel Pass at 3,793 feet, over which a road crosses the range. Within the mountains lie many valleys and numerous summer resorts. Winter sports and mountaineering are popular.

Bled, a fashionable romantic resort set northwest of Lyubljana on an idyllic small emerald green lake with a small island and baroque church in the center, has a dramatic castle towering overhead. To the northeast, the highest peaks of the Karavanke range form a natural boundary with Austria and the Julian Alps lie to the west. Bled has been a favorite destination for travelers for centuries.

Other points of interest are numerous castles; Kranjska Gora, a ski resort; Triglav National Park, a 210,000-acre nature preserve; Bohinj, a beautiful glacial lake with high mountains rising directly around it; the cities of Piran adorned with Gothic architecture, and Kobarid, the setting for Ernest Hemingway's *A Farewell to Arms*.

Because of their proximity to Italy and the fact that they were once part of the Austro-Hungarian Empire, Slovenes are fond of the food of these three countries. There are also Balkan influences. Specialties include chicken-noodle soup, fresh and saltwater seafood, spiced meat patties, pizzas, risotto, sausages, cheese-filled savory pastries, schnitzels, potato dumplings, *potica* (walnut roll), poppy seed and walnut-filled pastries, and desserts featuring cream with flavorings. Slovenes are particularly proud of their pastries and cakes.

The wine-growing regions of Slovenia are Podravje in the east, noted for several fine white wines; Posavje in the southeast that produces a light red wine; and the area around the coast that has a hearty red called Teran. Zganje is a favorite brandy distilled from a variety of fruits, most commonly plums, and the finest brandy is Pleterska Hruska made from pears.

Appetizers

In the Alpine countries a rich repertoire of marvelous morsels we call appetizers, served prior to a luncheon or dinner and at social gatherings, are tempting to the eye, pleasing to the palate, and stimulating to the appetite. Customarily one does not partake of prepandial libations without something to eat. Thus, whether a few or many, humble or luxurious, simple or complex, appetizers are carefully prepared and slowly savored.

The food served with drinks, or as a first course at the table, is light and delicate, planned to marry well with the menu to follow. This, however, is not always the case. In the Alpine cuisine there are a number of delectable appetizer presentations that are sort of a meal-before-the-meal.

The custom of serving and enjoying an elaborate galaxy of stimulating dishes with drinks before dining probably began in Europe. The French have traditionally enjoyed an assortment of hors d'oeuvres, including attractive filled pastries, rich salads, cold meats, pâtés, vegetable creations, and seafood dishes, as a prelude to luncheon. Today in private homes the fare may be a simple presentation of garnished canapés, olives, cheese sticks, little tarts, or a few raw vegetables with a flavorful dip, relished with an aperitif or glass of wine.

In Italy the well-known dazzling antipasto, a word meaning "before the meal," is a colorful and attractive array of some of the country's best and most popular fare. Among the specialties are raw and cooked vegetables, cured meats, seafood salads, sausages, olives, cheeses, and highly seasoned hot and cold prepared dishes. Whatever the choice, antipasto should offer a selection of little bites that reflects a diversion of flavors, textures, and colors.

For entertaining, the Austrians and Germans prepare attractive displays of *vorspeisen* "before foods" or appetizers. Enjoyed with *schnapps*, wine, or beer are a few selections or a copious spread of smoked fish, marinated herring, raw or pickled vegetables, several sausages, composed salads, filled pastries, and cheeses. In Switzerland, Liechtenstein, and Slovenia many of these same dishes, prepared according to local tastes, are also enjoyed as favorite before-the-meal delights.

While traveling in the Alpine countries it is always pleasurable to sample the regional appetizer delicacies, very often available only in season. This selection is representative of the various traditional dishes, and provides a choice of taste tempters that should prove a worthy and delectable overture to any meal.

Italian Ham with Fruit

In the Dolomites, a year-round mountain playground and dramatically beautiful part of northeastern Italy, one finds awe-inspiring scenery, opportunities for hiking and sports, and fine dining. Very often meals served at small hotels and inns in the mountain towns will begin with this refreshing first course or antipasto. It is made simply with prosciutto, a delicately dry cured pink ham that has a mild sweet flavor and has long been rated as one of Italy's great culinary contributions, served customarily with fresh melon or figs.

---

1 Crenshaw, cantaloupe, or honeydew melon, or fresh figs (2 per person), chilled

Thinly sliced prosciutto

Peel and seed the melon and cut into wedges. For each serving, offer 2 chilled melon wedges with 2 thin slices of the prosciutto placed over the top or to the side. For prosciutto with fresh figs, cut well-chilled fresh figs into halves or quarters. Arrange the slices of proscuitto next to them. Serve with a knife and fork.

White Bean and Tuna Salad

This easy-to-prepare antipasto is made with plump, tender white beans called cannellini and tuna fish, two favorite Italian foods.

4 cups drained, canned cannellini or other cooked white beans

½ cup minced onion

½ cup finely chopped fresh parsley

2 tablespoons fresh lemon juice

Salt and freshly ground pepper

1 can (7 ounces) tuna fish in oil, oil reserved

If canned beans are used, rinse quickly in cold water. In a large bowl combine the beans, onions, parsley, and lemon juice. Season with salt and pepper. Spoon onto a large plate. With a fork divide the tuna into chunks and arrange it over the bean mixture. Sprinkle with oil from the tuna fish. Serve cold.

Liptauer from Kitzbühel

4 to 6 servings

A favorite Austrian spread is made with a soft white cheese called Liptauer or Liptoi that originated in the Hungarian province of the same name. Now made in many variations, it usually includes several piquant seasonings and is served slathered on dark bread but it can also be a flavorful dip for raw vegetables. This is one that I recall enjoying at a small lakeside inn at the medieval town of Kitzbühel, a charming summer resort and fashionable winter sports center, the gateway to excellent ski slopes. Many of the picturesque buildings and gabled houses in the delightful Old Town date back to the sixteenth century when it was a prosperous mining town.

---

2 packages (3 ounces each) cream cheese, softened

¼ cup (½ stick) unsalted butter, softened

2 tablespoons capers, drained and chopped

1 tablespoon chopped chives

2 tablespoons chopped white or yellow onions

2 flat anchovy fillets, minced

2 teaspoons Dijon mustard

2 tablespoons paprika

Freshly ground pepper

In a large bowl cream the cheese and butter until smooth. Add the capers, chives, onions, anchovies, mustard, and paprika. Season with pepper. Mix to blend well. Shape into a mound on a serving plate. Chill, covered with plastic wrap, for 1 hour, up to 8 hours. Serve surrounded with thin pumpernickel slices or other dark bread.

Bruschetta with Tomatoes

4 servings

Wherever olive oil is made in Italy, the harvest is celebrated by drinking new young wine and eating bruschetta (broo-SKET-tah), or garlic bread. Prepared with thick slices of coarse-textured white bread toasted over a fire, rubbed with fresh garlic and drizzled with newly pressed brilliant greenish-gold olive oil, it has a memorable taste. Known also as fett'unta ("oily slice") and soma d'aj ("brushed with garlic"), among other names, it is traditionally eaten for breakfast or as a snack. The toasted bread has also become a popular appetizer or part of the antipasti selection. It's a perfect foundation for all sorts of marvelous toppings such as fried eggplant, anchovies, sausage slices, cheese spreads, freshly ground pepper and balsamic vinegar, and especially tomatoes either fresh or roasted.

---

4 thick (¾-inch) slices of firm-textured white bread

2 to 4 tablespoons extra-virgin olive oil

2 garlic cloves, halved

2 large tomatoes, sliced about thick ½-inch thick

4 slices mozzarella cheese

Fresh green herbs (thyme, basil, mint, parsley)

Salt

Preheat the oven to 450 degrees.

Grill or toast the slices of bread until lightly browned. While hot, drizzle one side of each slice with oil and rub with garlic. Arrange on a baking sheet, oil side up. Top with the tomato and cheese slices. Sprinkle with the herbs and salt. Bake for 3 to 4 minutes, until the cheese is melted. Serve at once.

Steak Tartare

2 servings

In the Alpine regions of Austria and Germany a favorite appetizer is steak tartare, raw ground beef combined with egg yolks and seasonings. Most often the mound of raw beef is served on individual plates to be combined to taste by each person. For parties or buffets, all the ingredients can be mixed beforehand and then served on a wooden board, tray, or platter, surrounded by bread and butter. The name of the dish is believed to have derived from the Tartar practice of scraping and eating raw meat. Purists still maintain that this is the best method of obtaining meat for the appetizer. Ground beef, however, is excellent but should be freshly ground at least twice and served as soon as possible.

½ pound ground lean boneless round or sirloin steak

2 egg yolks

Garnishes: 2 table-spoons finely chopped onions; 2 tablespoons capers, drained; 8 flat anchovy fillets, drained; 2 table-spoons chopped fresh parsley; 2 tablespoons freshly ground pepper

Divide the beef into 2 portions and shape each one into a mound. Place in the center of individual plates. Make a small depression in the center of each mound; carefully drop an egg yolk into each. Serve the garnishes in small individual saucers. Each person combines the beef and garnishes according to taste at the table.

Mount Triglav Yogurt-Vegetable Dip

This colorful nutritious dip is made with raw vegetables and plain yogurt, once called the milk of eternal life, but actually healthful cultured milk, low in butterfat and calories. Yogurt has long been a staple food in Slovenia where one of the major attractions is the nation's highest peak, Mount Triglav, dominating the northwest region of mountain and lakeside resorts with thermal springs and spas. Here also is the Triglav National Park, a 210,000-acre nature preserve noted for r its spectacular Alpine landscape with craggy mountain peaks, dense forests, and river gorges hundreds of feet deep.

---

2 cups plain yogurt

1 or 2 garlic cloves, crushed

2 tablespoons Dijon mustard

½ cup chopped scallions, with some green tops

2 tablespoons capers, drained and chopped

¼ cup finely chopped fresh parsley

Salt and freshly ground pepper

In a serving bowl or dish combine the yogurt, garlic, mustard, scallions, capers, and parsley. Season with salt and pepper. Refrigerate, covered with plastic wrap for at least 2 hours and up to 6 hours, to blend the flavors.

Triesenberg Salami Canapés

Makes about 1¾ cups

In the village of Trisenberg, 3,000 feet high in the Liechtenstein Alps where pine forests stretch toward the Alpine peaks, the unique history of this Walser community is documented in the folklore museum and reflected in its Valaisan-style houses. Favorite local specialties include those made with a variety of local sausages including salami.

---

1 cup finely chopped salami

6 tablespoons unsalted butter, softened

1 tablespoon minced yellow onion

2 tablespoons minced dill pickle

½ teaspoon paprika

Salt and freshly ground pepper

In a medium bowl combine the salami, butter, onions, pickle, and paprika. Season with salt and pepper. Refrigerate for at least 1 hour, and up to 6 hours to blend the flavors. Serve on small crusty rolls cut in half crosswise.

Italian Stuffed Mushrooms

Of the many Alpine mushroom creations, some of the most popular are mushroom caps stuffed with various fillings. The caps may be raw, boiled, baked, or broiled and eaten hot or cold. Some fillings are simple such as cheese and butter; others are more complicated preparations made with seafood or meats.

---

1 pound large mush-
  rooms

1 garlic clove, crushed

1 cup minced cooked
  ham

2 tablespoons finely
  chopped fresh
  parsley

2 tablespoons grated
  Parmesan cheese

2 tablespoons fine dry
  bread crumbs

Salt and freshly
  ground pepper

Olive oil

Preheat the oven to 350 degrees. Grease a shallow baking dish.

Clean and dry the mushrooms. Pull off the stems and reserve for another dish. In a medium bowl, combine the garlic, ham, parsley, grated cheese, and bread crumbs. Season with salt and pepper. Spoon the mixture into mushroom caps; sprinkle with oil. Arrange in the prepared dish. Bake for 20 minutes. While the mushrooms are cooking, sprinkle more oil over the stuffing so it will not be too dry. Serve hot.

Savoy Seafood Mushrooms

4 to 6 servings

Savoy, crowned by the icy splendor of Mont Blanc, is one of the most dramatic French provinces where vacationers have long enjoyed scenic attractions and culinary specialties. It has exceptional freshwater fish, wild birds, and mushrooms from Alpine forests. This is also dairy country, the source of superb creams, butter, and cheeses.
This specialty is adapted from a dish served at a local mountain inn in Savoy.

---

1 pound extra-large
  mushrooms

About ½ cup
  (1 stick) unsalted
  butter

¼ cup minced
  scallions

⅓ cup minced cooked
  seafood (shrimp,
  crab, tuna)

⅛ teaspoon freshly
  grated nutmeg

Salt and freshly
  ground pepper

1 tablespoon chopped
  fresh chives or
  parsley

Preheat the oven to 350 degrees.

Clean and dry the mushrooms. Pull off the stems and mince. In a medium skillet melt 4 tablespoons of the butter over medium-high heat. Add the scallions; sauté 3 minutes. Add the seafood and nutmeg. Season with salt and pepper and add the chives. Mix well and cool.

Melt 2 tablespoons of the butter and brush mushroom caps generously. Arrange in a shallow baking dish. Bake 15 to 20 minutes, until just tender. Fill with the seafood mixture, sprinkling each top with a little melted butter. Return to the oven. Bake 5 minutes longer. Serve with forks.

Interlaken Cheese-Onion Tart

6 servings

The timeless Victorian resort town of Interlaken is situated, as the name implies, between the stunning lakes of Thun and Brienz. It is from here that one gets a marvelous view of the Jungfrau (13,670) in all its splendor. As a gateway to the Berner Oberland the town has long been famous for its grand hotels including the Victoria-Jungfrau where Mark Twain once sojourned, restaurants, tearooms, and small inns where this Swiss favorite is a specialty.

Pastry for one 9-inch pie

3 tablespoons unsalted butter

3 large yellow onions, peeled and thinly sliced

1 tablespoon all-purpose flour

2 cups light cream or milk

4 eggs, beaten

2 cups grated Emmentaler or Swiss cheese

Salt and freshly ground pepper

Preheat oven to 375 degrees. Fit the prepared crust into a 9-inch pie pan.

In a medium skillet melt the butter over medium-high heat. Add onion slices; sauté until translucent, about 7 minutes. Stir in the flour and 1 cup of the cream. Cook, stirring, for 1 minute. Turn into a large bowl. Add the remaining 1 cup of cream, beaten eggs, and grated cheese. Season with salt and pepper. Mix well. Turn into the prepared pie shell, spreading evenly. Bake until the filling is set in the center and golden brown in spots, about 45 minutes. Remove from oven and cool on a wire rack. Serve warm or at room temperature.

Pizza

Pizza is a traditional snack and appetizer in the Alpine countries. It originated as a peasant dish in Italy where leftover bread dough was flattened into a disc, coated with olive oil, and topped with various colorful and tasty foods. Now made usually with tomatoes and mozzarella cheese, the pizza is baked in a very hot oven until tender and softly crisp. The word pizza in Italian means "pie." Here are recipes for two favorite Alpine pizzas.

Stresa Sausage-Vegetable Pizza

4 to 6 servings

Stresa, Italy's garden-filled resort town on the western shore of Lake Maggiore, is a popular center for lake cruises, touring the region's other highlights, and enjoying views of the towering Swiss Alps to the north. One of the local specialties is pizza enjoyed with the local wine at a trattoria. *This colorful pizza, topped with green peppers, mushrooms, and Italian sausage is tasty and easy to prepare.*

2 tablespoons olive oil

1 medium green pepper, cut into slivers

1 small onion, peeled and sliced

1 can (4 ounces) sliced mushroom, drained

1 (12-inch) pizza crust, unbaked

2 cups canned tomato sauce

1/2 pound mozzarella cheese, shredded

1/2 pound cooked Italian sausage, thinly sliced

Preheat the oven to 425 degrees.

In a small skillet heat oil over medium-high heat. Add the green pepper, onion, and mushrooms. Sauté 5 minutes. Remove from the heat. Put pizza crust in a 12-inch pan. Spread with the tomato sauce. Top with the cheese, sausage, and sautéed vegetables. Bake 25 minutes, until the crust is golden and the filling is bubbling. To serve, cut into wedges.

Onion-Olive Pizza

This French version of pizza, called pissaladiera, is a specialty of Provence but is enjoyed also in the Alpine province of Dauphine, which extends from the Rhone River to the Italian frontier. A famous highway, the Route Napoleon, passes through this province and along the way there are several superb restaurants and a few informal dining places where one can enjoy this pizza.

½ cup plus 1 tablespoon cup olive oil

2 tablespoons unsalted butter

8 medium yellow onions, peeled and thinly sliced (about 6 cups)

2 garlic cloves, crushed

Salt and freshly ground pepper

1 (12-inch) pizza crust, unbaked

1 can (2 ounces) flat anchovies, drained

12 large black olives, pitted

Preheat the oven to 425 degrees.

In a medium skillet heat the oil and butter over medium-high heat. Add the onions and garlic. Sauté about 5 minutes, until tender, being careful not to brown them. Remove from the heat. Season with salt and pepper; cool. Put the pizza crust in a 12-inch pan. Spread with the onion mixture. Make a lattice pattern with the anchovies over the onions. Place an olive in center of each square. Brush lightly with oil. Bake for about 25 minutes, until the crust is golden and the filling is bubbling.. Cool slightly. Cut into wedges.

Piedmontese Bagna Cauda

This hot dip for raw vegetables is a beloved specialty of northern Italy's Piedmont region. The name is from the Italian "hot bath" and the dish may be served as an appetizer. In Italy it is often enjoyed as a snack, or on Christmas Eve, as a whole meal. Generally the ingredients include a fair amount of olive oil, butter, chopped garlic, and anchovies. Delectable but rare, thinly sliced white truffles are also sometimes added. Some variations include heavy cream. For the vegetables, Italians like to include the cardoon, a relative of the artichoke. The sauce is kept warm over a spirit lamp or candle warmer in a chafing dish or small earthenware casserole. An electric hot tray can also be used.

½ cup (1 stick) unsalted butter

½ cup olive oil

2 to 4 garlic cloves, minced

8 anchovy fillets, drained and minced

1 canned white truffle, finely chopped (optional)

1 cup heavy cream

Assortment of raw vegetables: carrot sticks, scallions, green pepper strips, cucumber or zucchini slices, small whole mushrooms

In a medium saucepan combine the butter and oil over medium-low heat. Add the garlic; sauté briefly, stirring with a wooden spoon. Add the anchovies and truffle. Gradually add the cream, stirring constantly, being careful not to boil it. When heated, pour the dip into a chafing dish or small casserole and put over a spirit lamp or candle warmer to keep warm. Serve with the prepared raw vegetables to dip into the warm sauce.

Pan Bagna

This flavorful Provencal sandwich is called pan bagnat *or* pain baigne.
The name means "bathed bread," as the bread is bathed in olive oil.
It's an excellent sandwich for a picnic or mountain meal.

---

6 hard-crusted French
  rolls

½ cup olive oil

3 medium tomatoes,
  peeled and sliced

1 large red onion,
  peeled and sliced

1 can (2 ounces) flat
  anchovy fillets,
  drained

2 tablespoons red
  wine vinegar

2 garlic cloves,
  minced

Salt and freshly
  ground pepper

6 lettuce leaves,
  washed and dried

3 hard-cooked eggs,
  sliced

1 large green pepper,
  cut into strips

12 ripe olives, pitted
  and halved

Split the rolls horizontally. Drizzle the cut sides with the oil and let stand 10 minutes. Arrange the tomato slices on the bottom halves of the rolls. Top with onion slices and anchovy fillets. Sprinkle with vinegar, garlic, salt, and pepper. Place the lettuce leaves on the top halves of the rolls. Top with the egg slices, peppers, and olives. Sprinkle with salt and pepper. Carefully place the tops of the rolls on the bottoms and press down gently. For picnics, wrap the sandwiches in foil or plastic.

Cuisines of the Alps

Mushroom Salad Italiano

4 to 6 servings

Raw mushrooms are excellent in salads. They may be added to mixed greens, marinated in sour cream or well-seasoned dressings, or, as in this Alpine favorite, served with a flavorful vinaigrette. Serve as a luncheon first course or with olives, raw vegetables, hard-cooked egg wedges, and salami slices as an antipasto.

1 pound fresh mush-
rooms

⅓ cup olive oil

Juice of 2 lemons

2 garlic cloves,
minced or crushed

Salt and freshly
ground pepper

3 tablespoons
chopped fresh herbs
(basil, tarragon,
parsley, or dill)

3 tablespoons
chopped chives or
scallions

4 flat anchovy fillets,
drained and
chopped

2 medium tomatoes,
peeled and cut into
wedges

Clean the mushrooms by rinsing them quickly or wiping with wet paper towels to remove any dirt. Cut off any tough stem ends. Wipe dry and slice lengthwise. Place in a serving dish and add the oil, lemon juice, and garlic. Season with salt and pepper. Marinate at room temperature for 1 hour. Serve sprinkled with the herbs, and chives, and garnish with anchovies and tomato wedges.

German Sausage-Sauerkraut Sandwich

Serves 6

Bratwurst or frankfurters in toasted rolls are topped with beer-flavored sauerkraut to make savory sandwiches for an informal meal or snack.

1 tablespoon unsalted butter or vegetable oil

1 medium yellow onion, peeled and minced

1 can (1 pound) sauerkraut, drained

2 tablespoons beer

¼ teaspoon celery seed

Salt and freshly ground pepper

½ cup minced green pepper

6 frankfurter rolls, toasted

2 tablespoons spicy mustard

6 bratwurst or frankfurters, cooked and kept warm

In a medium saucepan melt the butter or heat the oil over medium-high heat. Add the onion and sauté for 4 minutes, stirring with a fork. Add the sauerkraut and sauté, stirring with a fork for 5 minutes. Mix in the beer and celery seed. Season with salt and pepper. Cook slowly, covered for 25 minutes. Add the green pepper 5 minutes before the cooking is finished. Spread the toasted rolls with mustard. Put a bratwurst in each roll. Spoon the hot sauerkraut mixture over each.

Croute au Fromage

This ham and cheese sandwich may be spread with butter and grilled or dipped in a batter and fried. It is a popular snack in Alpine countries.

---

4 slices firm white bread, buttered

4 thin slices cooked ham

4 slices Emmental or Gruyère cheese

4 eggs, fried and kept warm

Preheat the broiler.

Cover each slice of buttered bread with a slice of ham and cheese. Place in an ovenproof dish. To cook, place under the broiler until the cheese is bubbly and melted, a few minutes. Top each sandwich with an egg; serve at once.

Soups

A wealth of imaginative and diverse soups that can be relished with great delight on any occasion have emerged from the kitchens of the Alpine countries. Over the centuries, cooks have utilized the bounty of land and sea to create a marvelous repertoire of national favorites, prepared and flavored according to local taste. Indeed, there is nothing more rewarding at mealtime, or in between than a nourishing soup, an important mainstay of the everyday diet in many Alpine homes.

Soup making has long been an essential accomplishment and laudable art and soups were among man's earliest culinary creations. In Alpine countries from the earliest times and even up to the eighteenth century it was not easy to distinguish between gruels, brews, broths, potages (all words commonly used for soups), and soups. All were nourishing and usually thickened with grains or breads.

The English word soup evolved from the French *soupe*, which is of Germanic origin. It came directly from *sop* or *sopp*, the name for a piece of bread served or dipped in roast drippings, broth, or another liquid. Eventually the broth or liquid, as well as the bread, was called *sop* or *soupe*, and other ingredients were added.

In the cuisine of the Alpine countries there are still many similar words. In Austria and Germany and some areas of Switzerland, for example, the dish is *suppe*. The Italians use the word *zuppa* for some kinds of soup, and the French likewise designate one category as *soupe*, a heartier dish than the more frequently used potage.

Supposedly the number of *sops*, or pieces of bread, once served in soup was taken by guests as an indication of their host's stinginess or generosity.

The famous French chef, Auguste Escoffier, introduced notable changes in the preparation and presentation of soups and wrote extensively about them. He customarily, dined, however, on a light meal of soup with a sprinkling of rice and fruit. Cooks in other European nations also created excellent soups that were generally hearty and robust. For centuries many of the substantial varieties have traditionally constituted full meals in many homes. Some soups are also eaten as snacks or in the wee hours of the morning as a restorative or effective remedy after a night of celebrating.

Suffice it to say that soups are very important throughout the countries of the Alps. Recipes and descriptive data in this chapter will reveal national favorites and differences, but the marvelous collection will also attest to some laudable words of Escoffier. "Soup," he wrote, "puts the heart at ease, calms down the violence of hunger, eliminates the tensions of the day, and awakens and refines the appetite." The pleasure of enjoying soup is for everyone who sits at your table.

Minestrone

In the Italian Alps one of favorite specialties, relished particularly after a day of winter sports, is the thick vegetable soup called minestrone. The ingredients vary greatly, but there are usually a number of vegetables as well as pasta. The name derives from the Latin for "hand-out." Long ago monks kept pots of the soup on their monastery stoves to hand out to hungry wayfarers. Here is one version of the friars' soup.

3 thin slices bacon, chopped

1 tablespoon olive oil

1 large yellow onion, peeled and chopped

3 leeks, white parts only, cleaned and thinly sliced

1 or 2 garlic cloves, crushed

1 large carrot, peeled and diced

2 cups chopped green cabbage

2 small zucchini, stemmed and sliced

1 can (I pound) tomatoes, undrained and chopped

1½ cups diced raw peeled potatoes

8 cups beef bouillon or water

Salt and freshly ground pepper

1 can (I pound) white or kidney beans, drained

1 cup small pasta or broken-up spaghetti

Parmesan cheese, preferably freshly grated

In a pot combine the bacon, oil, onion, leeks, and garlic over medium-high heat and sauté 5 minutes. Add the carrot and cabbage and sauté for 5 minutes. Add the zucchini, tomatoes, potatoes, and bouillon. Bring to a boil. Season with salt and pepper. Reduce the heat to medium-low. Cook slowly, covered, about 30 minutes, until the vegetables are tender. Add the beans and pasta and cook about 12 minutes longer, until the pasta is tender. Serve with the grated Parmesan.

Soupe au Pistou

This favorite soup of France's lovely Provence and Alpine regions is very similar to mine-strone, but it includes a flavorful sauce, pistou, made of crushed garlic, olive oil, grated cheese, and fresh basil, which is added at the end of the cooking. The French relish the soup in early spring when it is prepared with small fresh white beans. Dried white navy beans are a good substitute.

3 tablespoons unsalted butter or olive oil

1 large yellow onion, peeled and diced

2 leeks, white parts only, trimmed, washed, and thinly sliced

2 large tomatoes, peeled and chopped

Salt and freshly ground pepper

2 cups diced raw potatoes

2 cups cut-up green beans

2 medium zucchini, diced

1 can (l pound) cannellini or navy beans, drained

½ cup broken spaghettini or vermicelli

3 garlic cloves, crushed or minced

½ cup chopped fresh basil or 1½ tablespoons dried basil

½ cup freshly grated Parmesan cheese

¼ cup olive oil

In a pot melt the butter or heat the oil over medium-high heat. Add the onion and leeks and sauté for 5 minutes. Add tomatoes; cook 3 minutes. Pour 3 quarts of water. Bring to a boil. Season with salt and pepper. Add the potatoes and green beans. Reduce the heat to medium-low and cook, uncovered, 15 minutes. Add the zucchini, cannellini, and spaghettini. Cook another 15 minutes, until all the vegetables are tender.

Meanwhile, prepare the *pistou* sauce. Pound the garlic and basil together to form a paste in a mortar with a pestle or mash them in a bowl with a wooden spoon. Stir in the cheese. Add the olive oil, l tablespoon at a time, beating to make a thick paste. Just before serving, add 2 cups of hot soup to the paste. Slowly stir the basil mixture into the hot soup. Serve at once. Pass the Parmesan cheese with the soup.

Bern Onion-Cheese Soup

This is a favorite soup in the Berner Oberland, a rugged region famous for panoramas of the Eiger, Monch, and Jungfrau mountains as well as dramatic scenery of deep gorges, waterfalls, and crystalline lakes. Many of region's hearty meals begin with this substantial soup featuring two of Switzerland's typical foods, onions and cheese.

---

3 tablespoons unsalted butter, plus ¾ cup, melted

3 tablespoons vegetable oil

About 1½ pounds yellow onions, peeled and thinly sliced (about 5 cups)

1 teaspoon sugar

6 cups beef bouillon

Salt and freshly ground pepper

½ cup dry white wine

6 or more slices crusty white bread, toasted

1¼ cups grated Gruyère or Emmental cheese

Preheat the oven to 375 degrees.

In a large saucepan heat the butter and oil over medium-high heat. Add the onions and sauté until translucent, about 8 minutes. Add the sugar. Pour in the bouillon. Season with salt and pepper. Bring to a boil. Reduce the heat to medium-low. Cook, covered, 20 minutes. Then add the wine and continue cooking for 10 minutes. Ladle the soup into earthenware or other ovenproof bowls. Top with one or more slices of toasted bread. Sprinkle generously with cheese and then with melted butter. Put the soup in the preheated oven for 20 minutes, until the cheese is melted. Then put under a heated broiler for a few minutes, until golden and crusty on top.

Pasta and Peas in Broth

6 to 8 servings

The Italians are fond of numerous kinds of brodi (broths or bouillons) made with meat, poultry, fish, or vegetables and enriched with colorful vegetables and tiny pasta. There is a saying in the Piedmont region that even a man condemned to prison should not be refused a cup of broth for it is a local specialty.

---

2 tablespoons unsalted butter

½ cup minced onion

1 garlic clove, crushed

8 cups chicken or vegetable broth

Salt and freshly ground pepper

1 package (10 ounces) frozen green peas

½ cup tiny pasta or broken spaghetti

Parmesan cheese, grated

In a pot melt the butter over medium-high heat. Add onion and garlic and sauté for 5 minutes. Add the broth and season with salt and pepper. Bring to a boil. Add the peas and cook, uncovered, until just tender, about 10 minutes.

Meanwhile, cook the pasta in boiling salted water until just tender; drain. Add the pasta to the soup and reduce the heat to medium-low. Cook for 5 minutes. Serve with grated Parmesan cheese.

Goulash

Goulash or gulyás soup, a Hungarian specialty popular in Austria and Slovenia, is flavorful and rich and good for a late evening supper after a day of skiing on the slopes. Some versions are made with potatoes but this one, more typical in the Alps, includes pasta.

- 3 tablespoons unsalted butter
- 2 large yellow onions, peeled and chopped
- 2 to 3 tablespoons paprika
- 2 pounds beef chuck or round, cut into l-inch cubes
- 3 tablespoons tomato paste
- 6 cups beef bouillon
- 1 tablespoon red wine vinegar
- Salt
- 2 cups egg noodles

In a large saucepan melt the butter over medium-high heat. Add the onions and sauté until translucent, 5 minutes. Add the paprika and cook 1 minute. Add beef and brown on all sides. Mix in the tomato paste and pour in the bouillon and vinegar. Season with salt. Lower the heat to medium-low. Cook, covered, about $1\frac{1}{4}$ hours, until the beef is tender.

Meanwhile, cook the noodles in boiling salted water until just tender. Add them to the soup before serving. Leave on the stove 5 minutes.

Chicken Soup with Noodles

8 to 10 servings

This is a good Slovenian one-dish meal for a weekend supper. It includes peas and mushrooms as well as noodles.

1 stewing chicken (about 4 pounds), cut up

1 bouquet garni (parsley sprigs, thyme, basil)

Salt and freshly ground pepper

1 cup fresh green peas

1 large green pepper, chopped

1 cup chopped fresh mushrooms

1 package ($\frac{1}{2}$ pound) fine egg noodles

2 tablespoons unsalted butter

2 tablespoons chopped fresh chives

Put the chicken, 4 quarts water, and the bouquet garni in a pot over medium-high heat. Season with salt and pepper and bring to a boil. Skim, reduce heat to medium-low, and cook, covered, about $1\frac{1}{2}$ hours, until the chicken is tender. With tongs remove the chicken from the broth. When cool enough to handle, remove the meat from the bones, discarding the skin and bones. Shred or cut up the chicken and return the pieces to the broth. Add the peas, green pepper, and mushrooms. Cook slowly, covered, 25 minutes. Add noodles during the last 10 minutes of cooking. Stir in the butter and chives just before removing from heat.

Austrian Beef-Vegetable Soup

8 to 10 servings

The favorite Austrian soup is rindsuppe, which serves several culinary roles. After cooking, the meat and vegetables can be taken out of the broth and served as a meal. The broth is then strained and clarified and used to enrich other dishes or is served by itself as a clear bouillon.

2 to 2 ½ pounds beef bones, cracked

3 pounds soup beef, such as chuck

3 tablespoons unsalted butter or vegetable oil

Salt and freshly ground pepper

1 large yellow onion, peeled and thinly sliced

2 medium leeks, white parts only, cleaned and thinly sliced

2 medium carrots, peeled and thinly sliced

1 celeriac (celery root), peeled and cubed

3 small turnips, peeled and cubed

2 cups cut-up cauliflower

4 sprigs parsley

2 medium bay leaves

½ teaspoon dried thyme

Scald the bones in boiling water and then rinse in cold water. Wipe the beef dry. In a pot melt the butter or heat the oil over medium-high heat. Add the beef and brown on all sides. Add the bones and 3 quarts water. Season with salt and pepper. Slowly bring the soup to a full simmer. Skim off any scum from the top. Cook over low heat, partly covered, 1½ hours. Again, remove any scum from the top. Add the onion, leeks, carrots, celeriac, turnips, cauliflower, parsley, bay leaves, and thyme. Continue cooking until the vegetables and meat are tender, about 1 hour longer. Remove and discard the parsley and bay leaves. Take out the meat and cut into bite-size pieces, discarding any bones or gristle. Return the meat to the soup.

Slovenian Sauerkraut Soup

It is commonly believed in Slovenia that this flavorful, nutritious soup will alleviate the aftereffects of imbibing too liberally. Thus, this very popular specialty is called "hangover soup" or "tipplers' soup."

¼ cup bacon fat or vegetable oil

1 large yellow onion, peeled and chopped

1 tablespoon paprika

3 cups finely chopped sauerkraut, drained

1 garlic clove, crushed

½ pound smoked sausage, sliced

Salt and freshly ground pepper

1 tablespoon all-purpose flour

3 tablespoons chopped fresh dill

1 cup sour cream, at room temperature

In a pot heat the bacon fat over medium-high heat. Add the onion and sauté until translucent, 4 minutes. Stir in the paprika and sauté for 1 minute. Add the sauerkraut and sauté, mixing with a fork, for 1 minute. Add the garlic and sausage. Season with salt and pepper and add 6 cups water. Reduce the heat to medium-low and cook, covered, for 30 minutes. Stir the flour and dill into the sour cream and add to the soup. Cook, stirring, until thickened and smooth.

Bavarian Beer Soup

Soups made with light or dark beer or ale have long been popular in Bavaria where they may be clear or creamy, hot or cold. Some include slices or cubes of pumpernickel or rye bread. Beer soups are not to everyone's taste, but there are many who like them. This one is easy to prepare and fun to serve for an informal meal.

2 (12-ounce) cans beer

1 tablespoon fresh lemon juice

2 teaspoons sugar

1 small stick cinnamon

1 or 2 whole cloves

2 teaspoons cornstarch

In a large saucepan combine the beer, lemon juice, sugar, cinnamon, and cloves over medium-high heat. Bring to a boil. Dissolve the cornstarch in 2 teaspoons cold water. Add it to the soup. Reduce the heat to medium-low and cook slowly, stirring, 3 or 4 minutes. Remove and discard the cinnamon and cloves. Serve at once.

Bean Soup with Cheese

In Liechtenstein's lovely old village of Steg, located down a winding road in the country's southern Alpine region, wooden chalets serve as holiday homes. Here the robust fare includes marvelous soups, including those featuring beans and cheese.

---

2 cups (1 pound) dried white beans

½ cup olive oil

1 large yellow onion, peeled and chopped

2 garlic cloves, crushed

1 large carrot, peeled and diced

2 stalks celery, with leaves, cleaned and chopped

1 cup diced cooked ham

⅛ teaspoon ground red pepper

1 tablespoon crumbled dried rosemary

Salt and freshly ground black pepper

½ cup finely chopped fresh parsley

8 to 10 slices crusty white bread, toasted

½ cup grated Parmesan cheese, preferably freshly grated

Wash and pick over the beans. Put into a pot and cover with water. Bring to a boil over medium-high heat boil for 2 minutes. Remove from the heat and let stand, covered, 1 hour. Drain the beans, reserving the cooking water. Add enough fresh cold water to make 3 quarts.

In a pot heat the olive oil over medium-high heat. Add the onion, garlic, carrot, celery, and ham and sauté for 5 minutes. Add the beans with water, ground red pepper, and rosemary. Season with salt and black pepper. Bring to a boil, then reduce the heat to medium-low. Cook slowly, partially covered, about 1½ hours, until the beans are tender. Remove about half the beans from the soup and purée them in a blender or food processor. Return the puree to the soup. Add the parsley and simmer, stirring, for 1 or 2 minutes. Put the toast in bottom of individual soup bowls. Ladle the soup over the toast. Serve at once. Pass the Parmesan cheese to sprinkle over the soup.

Slovenian Vegetable Soup

6 servings

This characteristic soup from the Julian Alpine region of Slovenia has an appealing tart flavor. It's excellent served with sandwiches for a winter luncheon.

⅓ cup unsalted butter

5 large yellow onions, peeled and chopped

5 cups beef bouillon

3 tablespoons cleaned and chopped leeks, white parts only

1 large potato, peeled and diced

Salt and freshly ground pepper

3 tablespoons red or white wine vinegar

2 teaspoons sugar

2 tablespoons finely chopped fresh parsley

1 cup sour cream, at room temperature

In a large saucepan melt the butter over medium-high heat. Add onions; sauté until translucent, about 6 minutes. Add the bouillon, leeks, and potato. Season with salt and pepper. Reduce heat to medium-low. Cook, covered, until the onions and potato are tender, about 30 minutes. Purée the mixture in a food processor and return to the saucepan. Add the vinegar and sugar. Stir in the parsley and sour cream. Mix well and heat through. Do not boil.

Bread Soups

From earliest times, simple soups have been prepared with various kinds of bread and in the Alpine countries there are many variations of this ancient dish that are interesting and delectable.

In France a soup made of bread and broth is known as a *panade*. It is generally a homely dish of stock or water, or perhaps another liquid, thickened with stale slices or cubes of firm crusty white bread, to which butter, salt, pepper, and a beaten egg might be added. Some old recipes also include other ingredients such as onions, leeks, garlic, or carrots, and flavorings like wine, herbs, or spices. The *panade* can be cooked on top of the stove or baked.

Elsewhere in the Alpine countries there are traditional preparations similar to the *panade*. The Austrians and Germans make bread soup with pumpernickel or rye bread and broth or beer to which onions or fruit such as apples are added. In Switzerland a traditional supper dish is made with alternate layers of bread and cheese, topped with cooked onions and bouillon, and then baked.

The Italians prepare some of the best bread soups. *Zuppa di fontina*, layers of bread and fontina cheese, covered with broth, is baked. Paradise Soup or *millefanti* is made with bread crumbs, grated Parmesan cheese, nutmeg, and eggs beaten into broth. Others are seasoned with garlic, herbs, tomatoes, and/or cheese, while an elaborate version includes bread rounds filled with ham and chicken.

Milk-Bread Soup

3 tablespoons unsalted butter

1 cup coarsely chopped stale bread

6 cups milk

1 tablespoon sugar

A dash of ground nutmeg

6 slices white bread, toasted

In a large saucepan melt the butter over medium-high heat. Add the chopped bread and fry until golden brown. Add the milk, sugar, and nutmeg. Reduce heat to medium-low and cook for 10 minutes or long enough to heat and blend the flavors. Serve in soup plates over slices of toasted bread.

German Pumpernickel Soup

6 servings

The Germans make several variations of brotsuppe, *bread soup, with pumpernickel or rye bread simmered in broth. This is a favorite Alpine version.*

6 slices stale pumpernickel, torn into pieces

8 cups beef bouillon, hot

2 tablespoons unsalted butter

1 medium yellow onion, peeled and chopped

Salt and freshly ground pepper

2 tablespoons chopped fresh parsley

½ cup sour cream, at room temperature

Paprika

In a large bowl cover the bread cubes with about 2 cups of the hot bouillon. Let it stand for about 10 minutes, until the bread is soft. In a large saucepan melt the butter over medium-high heat. Add the onion and sauté for 4 minutes. Add the bread mixture and remaining bouillon. Season with salt and pepper. Reduce the heat to medium-low and cook, covered, 25 minutes. Add the parsley. Serve the soup garnished with sour cream and paprika.

Italian Bread-Tomato Soup

⅓ cup olive oil

3 garlic cloves, crushed

4 medium tomatoes, peeled and chopped

6 cups chicken broth

1 bay leaf

⅛ teaspoon ground red pepper

Salt and freshly ground black pepper

6 thick slices crusty white bread, toasted

About ⅓ cup grated Parmesan cheese

In a large saucepan heat the oil over medium-high heat. Add the garlic and sauté for 1 minute. Add the tomatoes and sauté for 3 minutes. Pour in the broth. Add the bay leaf and ground red pepper. Season with salt and black pepper. Bring to a boil. Reduce the heat to medium-low and cook, covered, 25 minutes. Remove and discard the bay leaf. To serve, put a toasted slice of bread in each soup bowl and sprinkle with grated Parmesan cheese. Pour the soup into each bowl.

Egg and Cheese Dishes

Two of the most important basic Alpine foods are eggs and cheese that are made into nourishing and innovative dishes. Over the centuries these have not been treated as ordinary fare but have been accorded great respect, often reserved for more exotic viands. In the Alps, eggs, one of nature's almost perfect foods, are not only enjoyed as breakfast fare but are made into inventive specialties offered as entrées for luncheons or suppers.

Culinary experts have long been intrigued with perfecting egg cookery and there are fascinating controversies concerning all the basic egg techniques from boiling to poaching. Thankfully, Alpine cooks have long used traditional methods and simple preparations that are as cherished today as they were hundreds of years ago.

One of the best and most popular of the Alpine dishes is the omelet or *omelette*, a word taken from an old French word for a thin plate. It is an ancient dish, glorified and popularized by the French who have developed hundreds of superb recipes for making unsweetened and sweetened kinds. Omelets in various forms and ingeniously flavored, have become an element of almost all the Alpine cuisines.

The soufflé is another remarkable and renowned egg creation based on a thick sauce with the addition of beaten egg whites and flavorings. There are two types of soufflés, the unsweetened, which is served for luncheon, as a dinner first course, or for supper; and the sweetened, which is eaten for dessert. The word soufflé is from the French for "puffed up" and each one is a lovely inflated creation that has to be served immediately from the oven because it quickly deflates. Unsweetened soufflés may be made with cheese, vegetables, seafood, or meat.

While eggs and cheese marry well in many superb Alpine specialties, there are also a fascinating variety of innovative cheese dishes made with the local products of each country. The art of making cheese was known by the early Romans who are generally credited with spreading it to the rest of Europe.

After the fall of the Roman Empire, cheese-making knowledge was kept alive and further advanced in the monasteries of Western Europe. Made with the milk of cows, goats, sheep, or buffalo, cheeses were developed into the categories now universally known as very hard, hard, semisoft ripened, soft ripened, and soft unripened.

While France, Italy, Austria, Liechtenstein, Germany, and Slovenia all have notable cheese creations, since ancient times Switzerland has been known particularly for its incomparable rustic and full-flavored cheeses made in a land where milk, cream, and butter form an important part of the cuisine. Julius Caesar ordered that Swiss cheeses be sent to him over the Alps. For centuries the making of cheese has been an important village industry and a large part of the Swiss culture. Today it is a regionally controlled, cooperative effort with each area specializing in its own type of cheese.

What most people outside the country think of as "Swiss" cheese is the flavorful large, dense-textured kind with big holes or eyes that was made originally by "mountain people." Doubtless the greatest and best known is Emmental (EM-awn-TAHL), which originated in the lovely green and rolling valley of the Emme River in the canton of Bern. The largest of the Swiss cheeses, it is easily recognized by its large holes, dry and hard rind, light golden color, and sweet, nutty flavor. The mainstay of any tray of selected cheeses, it is ideal for fondue, sandwiches, and salads, as well as omelets and baked dishes. It also marries well with fruit and wine. Gruyère, named for the perfectly preserved medieval town of Gruyères, is not as large, has smaller holes and a pleasant assertive fruity flavor. Because it melts easily and smoothly, it is an excellent cheese for fondue, soups, and grilled cheese sandwiches. Its distinctive flavor also goes well with fruit.

Other excellent Swiss cheeses are appenzeller, or appenzell that has a golden yellow rind and curd, and a unique fruity or spicy tang that comes from a special mixture of pepper, herbs, and white wine or cider. It is a fine eating cheese and goes well with fruit and red wine. Sbrinz, the hardest and oldest Swiss cheese goes especially well in soups and sauces, and is often very thinly sliced to eat with bread. Vacherin is a variant of Gruyère, and Tete de Moine has a strong fruity flavor and aroma.

Cheeses, of course, are often eaten uncooked, either plain or with other foods such as fruit. In some countries they are standard breakfast foods as well as common snacks and desserts. The repertoire of cheese dishes includes sandwiches, omelets, soufflés, soups, salads, and pies, among others.

French Omelet

While traveling through the French Alpine regions it is a pleasure to order a simple omelette made with lightly beaten eggs and a minimum of seasoning that is delicate and delicious. An omelet may feature other ingredients such as cheese, minced onions, ham, mixed herbs, potatoes, fish, mushrooms, and cooked meats. It is not difficult to make a French omelet but it is best to closely follow the directions.

3 eggs

1 tablespoon cold
   water

Salt and freshly
   ground pepper

Unsalted butter

Break the eggs, one at a time into a medium bowl. Mix gently to combine the whites and yolks. Pour in the water. Season with salt and pepper. Stir until well mixed but do not overbeat. Warm an omelet pan or skillet over medium-low heat and brush the surface with butter. When the butter is sizzling, stir the egg mixture again and pour quickly into the pan. Mix with a fork and shake the pan back and forth. When the mixture begins to set, run a knife around the edge, tilting the pan to let the runny mixture in the center run toward the sides and under the center. When the omelet is set, fold the sides in toward the center. Turn out onto a warm plate or platter. Brush with melted butter, if desired. Serve at once.

Note: If desired, add 1 or 2 tablespoons of minced scallions, fresh herbs, grated cheese, or hopped cooked spinach to the egg mixture. Or sprinkle ⅓ cup of diced cooked potatoes, sautéed mushrooms, diced cooked ham, seafood, or vegetables over the eggs after they have set a little.

Italian Frittata

The traditional Italian omelet called frittata is quite different from the French one as it is cooked quickly on both sides and served flat instead of folded. Some are made only with eggs but most varieties include other ingredients such as chopped cooked meats, seafood, and especially vegetables—onions, potatoes, zucchini, spinach, asparagus, artichokes, mushrooms—and seasonings. This version has an appealing nutlike flavor and golden crust.

1 to 2 tablespoons unsalted butter

4 teaspoons olive oil

½ cup sliced scallions, with some tops

1 or 2 garlic cloves, crushed or minced

1 cup finely chopped cooked spinach, thoroughly drained

1 tablespoon minced fresh basil

⅓ cup grated Parmesan cheese

6 eggs, lightly beaten

Salt and freshly ground pepper

In an omelet pan or medium-size skillet heat the butter and oil over medium-high heat. Add the scallions and garlic and sauté for 3 minutes. Meanwhile, in a medium bowl combine the spinach, basil, Parmesan, and eggs, and season with salt and pepper. Mix well. Quickly pour the mixture into the pan, tilting to spread it evenly. Cook until the eggs are set and the bottom is golden and crusty. While cooking, loosen the edges to let any uncooked egg run underneath. Remove from the stove. Put a large plate over the pan; invert the frittata onto it. Lightly grease the pan and slide the frittata back into the pan, cooked side up. Cook 1 or 2 minutes. Remove to a warm plate and cut into wedges.

58   **Cuisines of the Alps**

Gardener's Omelet

4 to 6 servings

This Slovenian omelet, made with a variety of seasonal vegetables, is a typical Alpine dish, good for a luncheon or supper entrée.

---

4 slices thin bacon, diced

2 medium yellow onions, peeled and chopped

2 garlic cloves, crushed

1 cup diced carrots, cooked

1 cup cooked green peas

1½ cups diced cooked potatoes

8 eggs, lightly beaten

⅛ teaspoon cayenne pepper

Salt and freshly ground pepper

2 tablespoons finely chopped fresh parsley

In a medium skillet sauté the bacon, onions, and garlic over medium-high heat for 5 minutes. Pour off all the fat except 3 tablespoons. Add the carrots, peas, and potatoes and sauté for 2 minutes. Meanwhile, in a medium bowl combine the eggs and cayenne. Season with salt and pepper and stir in parsley. Add the eggs to the vegetable mixture. Cook until the mixture is set and the surface is dry. To serve, cut into wedges.

Egg and Cheese Dishes   **59**

Italian Artichoke Omelet

This baked omelet, tortino di carciofi, *is made with tender young artichokes which are particularly flavorful in Italy. Frozen artichoke hearts are used in this recipe as a substitute.*

1 (9-ounce) package frozen artichoke hearts, thawed

¼ cup olive oil

1 garlic clove, crushed

Salt and freshly ground pepper

2 tablespoons fresh lemon juice

8 eggs, lightly beaten

⅓ cup finely chopped fresh parsley

Preheat the oven to 400 degrees and grease a 10-inch pan.

Cut each artichoke heart in half lengthwise. In a medium skillet heat the oil over medium-high heat. Add the garlic and artichokes and sauté until fork-tender. Season with salt and pepper and add the lemon juice. Spoon the mixture into the prepared baking dish. In a medium bowl combine the eggs and parsley. Pour over artichoke mixture, tilting the pan to distribute the eggs evenly. Bake about 15 minutes, until the eggs are set. To serve, cut into wedges.

Fishermen's Omelet

Long ago wives of coastal fishermen along the Adriatic Sea created a hearty dish using leftover cooked fish and eggs that is still sometimes eaten in mid-morning as a second breakfast by early rising seafarers. The seasoning depends on what fresh herbs are available.

---

3 tablespoons olive or vegetable oil

6 scallions, with some tops, minced

2 tablespoons tomato paste

1 tablespoon lemon juice

⅛ teaspoon cayenne pepper

Salt and freshly ground pepper

2 cups diced cooked white fish

6 eggs, lightly beaten

3 tablespoons finely chopped fresh dill or parsley

In a medium saucepan heat the oil over medium-high heat. Add the scallions and sauté for 3 minutes. Stir in the tomato paste, lemon juice, and cayenne pepper. Season with salt and pepper and cook, uncovered, 5 minutes. Remove from the heat. Add the fish, eggs, and dill. Mix well. Pour into a well greased skillet over medium-low heat. Cook until the omelet is set and the top is dry, about 12 minutes. Fold in half. Serve at once.

French Mushroom Soufflé

4 servings

This elegant soufflé is an excellent entrée for a luncheon or supper in Alpine countries where fresh mushrooms are favorite foods.

¼ cup (½ stick) unsalted butter

1 tablespoon minced shallots or scallions

1 tablespoon lemon juice

1 cup finely chopped fresh mushrooms

⅛ teaspoon grated nutmeg

Salt and freshly ground pepper

3 tablespoons all-purpose flour

1 cup milk

4 eggs, separated, at room temperature

1 egg white, at room temperature

Preheat the oven to 375 degrees. Grease a 1½-quart soufflé dish or casserole.

In a small skillet, melt 1 tablespoon of the butter over medium-low heat. Add the shallots and lemon juice and sauté for 2 minutes. Add the mushrooms and sauté for 3 minutes. Add the nutmeg and season with salt and pepper. Remove from the heat.

In a medium saucepan melt the remaining 3 tablespoons butter over medium-low heat. Stir in the flour to form a roux and cook, stirring for 1 minute. Gradually add the milk, stirring continuously. Cook slowly until thickened and smooth. Remove from the heat and cool a little. Beat the egg yolks until creamy and stir into the white sauce. Add the mushroom mixture to the sauce. Beat the egg whites until stiff. Carefully fold half of them into the mushroom mixture. Then add the remaining half. Spoon the mixture into the prepared dish.

Bake 30 to 35 minutes, until puffed and golden. Serve at once.

Baked Eggs with Spinach and Yogurt

4 servings

This typical Slovenian midday dish is nourishing and tasty. Serve with crusty bread.

---

2 (10-ounce) packages
frozen chopped
spinach, thawed
and drained

8 eggs

2 garlic cloves,
crushed

1½ cups plain yogurt

½ cup grated
cheddar cheese

Salt and freshly
ground pepper

3 tablespoons minced
fresh parsley

Preheat the broiler. Grease an 8- or 9-inch shallow baking dish.

Spoon the cooked spinach into the prepared baking dish. With the back of a large spoon make 8 depressions in the spinach. Break 1 egg into each depression. In a medium bowl combine the garlic, yogurt, and cheese. Season with salt and pepper and spoon over the eggs. Sprinkle with chopped parsley. Broil about 5 minutes or until hot and bubbly. Serve at once.

Baked Eggs with Vegetables

4 servings

This is a typical Slovenian vegetable-egg entrée.

---

1 medium eggplant
(about 1 pound),
diced

1 cup olive oil

2 garlic cloves,
crushed

Salt and freshly
ground pepper

1 large yellow onion,
peeled and chopped

6 medium ripe
tomatoes, peeled
and chopped

1 teaspoon dried
oregano

8 eggs

½ cup finely chopped
fresh parsley

Preheat the oven to 350 degrees.

In a large skillet heat ½ cup of the oil over medium-high heat. Add 1 garlic clove and the eggplant, several pieces at a time. Fry until golden and soft, adding more oil as needed. Season with salt and pepper. Remove from the oil with a slotted spoon and put into a bowl; set aside.

Add the remaining 1 clove garlic and onion to the oil and sauté for 4 minutes. Add the tomatoes and oregano. Season with salt and pepper, mix well, and cook for 5 minutes. Spoon the eggplant into the center of a large shallow baking dish. Surround it with the tomato mixture. With the back of a large spoon make 8 depressions in the vegetable mixture. Break an egg into each depression. Sprinkle the eggs with parsley and bake about 12 minutes, until the eggs are set.

German Farmer's Breakfast

In Germany this hearty combination of potato and eggs called bauernfrühstuck *is a favorite midmorning second breakfast. The dish is a restaurant specialty as well as one commonly made in the home.*

---

6 thin slices bacon, diced

1 medium yellow onion, peeled and minced

8 medium waxy potatoes, peeled and cubed

6 eggs, lightly beaten

2 tablespoons finely chopped fresh parsley

Salt and freshly ground pepper

In a large skillet fry the bacon over medium-high heat until crisp. Remove from the pan and drain. Pour off all the bacon fat except 3 tablespoons. Add the onion to the pan and sauté for 4 minutes. Stir in the potatoes and cook until tender and golden.

Meanwhile, in a medium bowl combine the cooked bacon, eggs, and parsley. Season with salt and pepper and mix well. Pour over the potato-onion mixture. Reduce the heat to medium-low. Cook, occasionally slipping a knife around the edges to let any uncooked egg run under, until the eggs are set. When cooked, remove from the heat and cut into wedges.

Cheese Quiche

Quiche, believed to have originated in France's Lorraine region, is now an international favorite made in many variations. This is a good basic recipe used in Alpine regions.

Pastry for 1 (8- or 9-inch) pie

2 cups (½ pound) grated Gruyère or Swiss cheese

1 tablespoon all-purpose flour

4 eggs

2 cups light cream

⅛ teaspoon freshly grated nutmeg

Salt and freshly ground pepper

2 tablespoons unsalted butter

Preheat the oven to 400 degrees.

Place the ring from a springform pan on a baking sheet, or a straight-sided cake pan, and line it with the pastry dough. Flute the edge of the shell and prick the bottom with a fork. Place a layer of aluminum foil or heavy brown paper over the pastry and fill it with dried beans or rice to keep the pastry from shrinking while baking. Bake for 8 minutes. Remove the pastry shell from the oven and discard the paper and beans or rice. Prick the dough again with a fork and return it to the oven for about 2 minutes longer. Remove from the oven and cool.

Lower the oven temperature to 375 degrees. Combine the cheese and flour and spread evenly in the pastry shell. In a large bowl beat the eggs. Mix in the cream and nutmeg. Season with salt and pepper and pour over the cheese. Cut the butter into tiny pieces and distribute over the top. Bake for 25 to 35 minutes, until the custard is set and a knife inserted into the center comes out clean. Remove from the oven and let the quiche stand for 2 or 3 minutes. Remove the ring and slide the quiche onto a warm plate. Cut into wedges.

Swiss Raclette

Raclette, originally from the canton of Valais, is known all over Switzerland as a traditional country dish. The name derives from the French verb *racler*, "to scrape." It was originally made by holding or putting a large piece of cheese in front of an open fire and, as the cheese melted, scraping the melted surface off onto a warm plate. It was then eaten with boiled potatoes, pickled onions, gherkins, and freshly ground pepper. Today, it is done in front of a special electric grill. In Switzerland the preferred cheeses are the semifirm kinds from Valais, such as *Gosmer*, *Bagnes*, or *raclette*, semisoft and high in fat, making it particularly suitable for melting. The flavor is mild and rich. A good wine to serve with this dish is a chilled Valais Fendant.

The Swiss have improvised a substitute plan for anyone wishing to make *raclette* in the home, where an open fire or electric grill is not available. They suggest that a large piece of cheese be put in a hot oven (450 degrees) until it begins to melt. It can be then scraped and served on hot plates with the accompaniments mentioned above. Alternately, melt slices of cheese under the broiler and serve the same way.

Swiss Cheese Fondue

4 servings

The best known of Switzerland's great dishes, fondue is a gently bubbling pot of flavorful cheese into which one dips pieces of crusty white bread. The name comes from the French verb fondre, *meaning "to melt." Although its origins are not known, many believe that fondue was created by mountain villagers who melted pieces of hardened cheese with a little white wine in a pot over an open fire. Particularly appealing is the idea of do-it-yourself cookery, as the dish is placed in the middle of the table and diners dunk bread cubes into the aromatic creamy cheese mixture.*

The Swiss make fondue in a heavy flat-bottomed round dish with a handle which is called a caquelon. It can be earthenware or made of cast iron or other metal, but it has to be heavy to hold the heat. Possible substitutes are chafing dishes or casseroles. The dish is placed over heat such as a spirit-burner, candle, or other device that can be regulated during cooking. Also necessary are long-handled forks for spearing and dunking the bread cubes. Each piece of the bread should have some crust on it so it will not slip off the fork. (If this happens, the loser of the bread must forfeit a bottle of wine or kiss the person to his or her right.) Wine is very important in the dish; it should be a dry white wine with enough acid to help liquefy the cheese. Good Swiss wines are Fendant-Petillant or a Neuchâtel.

The choice of cheese is of utmost significance, for in order to achieve the proper consistency (not lumpy or stringy), it should be well matured. Fondue usually features a mix of Emmental and Gruyère, but other variations use different Swiss cheeses such as Vacherin or appenzeller. The preferred drink to serve with fondue is kirsch; or you may serve the same wine that was used in the dish. Generally speaking, it is best not to serve very cold or chilled drinks with the fondue. In Switzerland a course of smoked meats, followed by fresh fruit and tea, is served after the cheese dish. This recipe is for the traditional Neuchâtel fondue, which I first enjoyed in that lovely Swiss city.

1 garlic clove, cut in half

2 cups dry white wine

1 to 2 teaspoons fresh lemon juice (optional)

½ pound Emmental cheese, diced or shredded (2 cups)

½ pound Gruyère cheese, diced or shredded (2 cups)

1 tablespoon cornstarch

3 tablespoons kirsch, gin, or vodka

⅛ teaspoon grated nutmeg

Salt and freshly ground pepper

About 8 slices crusty white bread, cut into cubes

Rub the inside of a fondue dish or casserole with the garlic clove. Add the wine and lemon juice. Heat the mixture gradually over a low flame until the liquid begins to bubble. Add the cheeses, a little at a time, stirring constantly with a wooden spoon, until they melt. Dissolve the cornstarch in the kirsch and stir into the cheese mixture. Increase the heat to moderate. Continue cooking and stirring until the mixture is smooth and creamy. Add the nutmeg and season with salt and pepper. Keep the fondue bubbling over low heat while serving. If the mixture becomes too thick, gradually add some warm wine, stirring continuously, until it reaches the desired consistency. To serve, each person spears a small piece of bread with a long-handled fork and then dips it into the cheese mixture before eating.

Piedmont Fonduta

An Italian version of fondue called *fonduta* is a famous Piedmont dish made with one of Italy's great cheeses, fontina, named for Mount Font in the Valle d'Aosta. It is sweet, mild, and semisoft, pitted with tiny holes and melts well. *Fonduta* also includes beaten eggs or egg yolks, butter, light cream, salt, and pepper. It cooks gently until thick and creamy. It is then covered with very fine slices of raw white truffles, a remarkable addition imparting a characteristic flavor to the fontina cheese, a combination for which there is no substitute. It is served as a delicious hot antipasto or as a light luncheon or supper dish.

Fish

Among the great gastronomic pleasures of the Alpine countries, none is more fascinating and delightful than the superb seafood. A varied and bountiful harvest of fish and shellfish from both fresh and salt waters is readily available and the cookery enhances the natural qualities and versatility of this marine treasure trove.

Since the beginning of time man has relied on the waters of sleepy streams, gurgling brooks, fast-running rivers, placid ponds, tepid and icy lakes, and deep, mysterious seas to provide necessary, nutritious, and inexpensive food. Without these resources he would not have survived. It is most interesting that through the centuries this bounty has been utilized to provide not only daily sustenance but also notable and distinguished culinary creations.

An affinity for fish began in the Alpine regions with the early peoples who eagerly sought out the resources of inland waters and those of the neighboring seas. During the Middle Ages seafood became an important food, an essential supplement to the meager everyday diet. Quite understandably fishing became an important industry and pastime particularly in the Alpine rivers and lakes. What makes the fish superlative today is its incredible freshness.

For centuries, cooks have passed on the art of skewering firm-fleshed fish, grilling tender fillets, baking fish in paper, frying seafood in oil or butter, stuffing large fish with flavorful mixtures, baking whole ones on a bed of vegetables, or slowly stewing several kinds together to blend flavors.

In Alpine countries the lively and colorful fish markets are good places to observe the great variety of seafood. The markets contain myriad species, fresh from streams, lakes, or the sea, some familiar and others unknown, native to local waters.

Particularly noteworthy are perch, pike, salmon, and trout, caught in swift, cold mountain streams and served most often grilled, fried, *au bleu* or *meuniere*. Fishermen on Altaussee Lake in the Salzkammergut area of Styria's Eastern Alps set their nets for *saibling*, a pink-fleshed trout fried in butter and served at inviting lakeside restaurants. From France's Lake Leman comes a salmon-pink fish called *fera*, another rare delectable treasure.

One of the greatest Alpine piscatorial treasures is *omble chevalier*, which is of the salmon genus but resembles lake trout. Called "the finest and most delicate of freshwater fish," it is actually a saltwater fish living in fresh water, especially the deep lakes of Savoy and Switzerland. It has a curious history and strange name for a fish.

"If you have ever done any serious eating near the Alpine lakes of France and Switzerland, you must have tasted one of the most praised food fishes of the world, honored by the noble name of omble chevalier—the knightly omble," wrote Waverly Root. Its flesh is very delicate and in Switzerland it is usually poached in red or white wine with shallots or mushrooms.

While it is not possible to include recipes for all the inviting Alpine fish dishes, and indeed some of them cannot be duplicated outside the Alps because the species are not available, this selection is representative of the interesting repertoire.

Blue Trout

In several Alpine countries a favorite way to prepare fish is to marinate it briefly or cook it in a vinegar solution, which turns the skin a vivid blue. To prepare truite au bleu, *it is essential to have freshly caught trout, handled as little as possible before cooking. Prepared in this manner, it is particularly flavorful.*

4 whole (1-pound) trout, dressed

1 cup white vinegar

2 parsley sprigs, plus additional for garnish

2 tablespoons minced onion

1 bay leaf

Salt and freshly ground pepper

Lemon wedges, for garnish

Wash the trout under running water. If desired, form each fish into a ring by tying the head to the tail with a strong thread. In a pot combine the vinegar, 3 cups water, 2 parsley sprigs, the onion, bay leaf, salt, and pepper and cover. Bring to a boil and add the trout. Reduce the heat to medium-low and cook for 4 to 6 minutes until the fish is tender. Drain well. Serve garnished with parsley sprigs and lemon wedges.

Saas-Fee Trout With Mushroom Stuffing

6 servings

The spectacular little resort of Saas-Fee lying in a deep valley is encircled by fiercely glaciated peaks with 13 towering more than 13,000 feet. Among them is the Dom, 14,908 feet, the highest mountain standing entirely in Switzerland. The village is known for its wooden chalets, hotels, and fine restaurants featuring dishes based on local foods, including freshly caught trout stuffed with mushrooms.

---

6 whole trout, about 1 pound

Salt

¾ cup unsalted butter

½ cup sliced scallions, with some tops

2 cups sliced fresh mushrooms

1 tablespoon fresh lemon juice

4 cups small soft white bread cubes

½ teaspoon dried marjoram

¼ cup finely chopped fresh parsley

Freshly ground pepper

Preheat the oven to 350 degrees. Grease a shallow baking dish.

Wash the trout and pat dry. Sprinkle inside and out with salt. In a large skillet melt the butter over medium-high heat. Reserve ¼ cup of the melted butter and set aside. Add the scallions to the pan and sauté for 4 minutes. Add the mushrooms and lemon juice and sauté for another 4 minutes. Add the bread and cook until golden. Stir in the marjoram and parsley and season with salt and pepper. Spoon the stuffing into the fish cavities, closing them with small skewers. Arrange in the prepared baking dish. Brush with the reserved butter. Bake, about 25 minutes, or until fork-tender.

French Sole *Bonne Femme*

The name of this classic French fish specialty, which appears on the menus of many Alpine restaurants, means "good housewife." In gastronomic parlance, however, it refers to a dish that includes mushrooms and white wine.

1½ pounds sole fillets

Salt and freshly ground pepper

4 tablespoons unsalted butter

1 medium yellow onion, peeled and minced

1 garlic clove, crushed

½ pound mushrooms, cleaned and sliced

1 tablespoon fresh lemon juice

2 tablespoons finely chopped fresh parsley

½ cup dry white wine

1 teaspoon all-purpose flour

¼ cup light cream

Sprinkle the fillets with salt and pepper; set aside. In a small skillet melt 3 tablespoons of the butter over medium-high heat. Add the onion and garlic and sauté for 4 minutes. Using a slotted spoon, transfer the onion mixture to a large skillet over medium-high heat. Place the sole over the onion mixture. Add the mushrooms and lemon juice to the small skillet and sauté 4 minutes. Spoon the mushrooms over the fish, adding any liquid in the pan. Sprinkle with the parsley and pour wine around the fish. Bring to a boil, then reduce the heat to medium-low. Cook, covered, about 7 minutes, until the fish is tender. Add the remaining 1 tablespoon butter to the pan and stir in the flour. Gradually add the cream, and cook slowly, stirring constantly, until thickened. Serve at once.

Italian Fish Cooked In Paper

Fish cooked and served in paper is a great favorite in Italy and other Alpine countries. One of the best and most popular fish used in this type of cookery is the delicate red mullet, prized since ancient times for its particularly appealing flavor. Although there are many varieties of mullet, the two most common ones in Europe are the red and gray, both taken from saltwater.

Parchment paper or aluminum foil

3 tablespoons unsalted butter

4 tablespoons olive oil

2 medium yellow onions, peeled and finely chopped

2 garlic cloves, crushed

2 medium carrots, peeled and diced

2 medium celery stalks, cleaned and diced

½ cup finely chopped fresh parsley

Salt and freshly ground pepper

4 small red mullets, or other white fish, cleaned, washed, and dried

Preheat the oven to 450 degrees. Cut 4 pieces of parchment paper or foil large enough to completely enclose each of the fish.

In a small skillet melt the butter with 2 tablespoons of the oil over medium-high heat. Add the onions and garlic and sauté for 4 minutes. Add the carrots and celery and sauté for 2 minutes. Stir in the parsley and season with salt and pepper. Remove from the heat.

Place each fish on a piece of parchment or foil. Spoon the vegetable mixture over the fish, dividing it evenly. Sprinkle with the remaining 2 tablespoons oil. Fold over the paper to enclose the ingredients completely and crinkle the edges to secure them. Place on a baking sheet. Bake about 15 minutes, until the fish is tender. Serve the fish in the paper, to be opened at the table.

Mushroom-Stuffed Pike

4 to 6 servings

This is an interesting way of preparing pike that is common in Germany and Austria.

---

1 whole (4- to 5-pound) pike, washed

Salt

3 tablespoons unsalted butter

½ cup minced scallions, with some tops

1 pound mushrooms, cleaned and sliced

2 tablespoons fresh lemon juice

Freshly grated nutmeg

Freshly ground pepper

2 cups small stale white bread cubes

3 tablespoons finely chopped fresh dill or parsley

1 cup dry white wine

1 cup sour cream, at room temperature

Preheat the oven to 350 degrees. Grease a shallow baking dish large enough to hold the fish.

Sprinkle the pike inside and out with the salt. In a medium skillet melt the butter over medium-high heat, add the scallions and sauté for 2 minutes. Add the mushrooms and lemon juice and sauté for 4 minutes. Season with nutmeg, salt, and pepper. Stir in the bread cubes and dill. Remove from the heat and stuff the mixture into the cavity of the fish. Close the cavity with small skewers. Place the pike in the prepared baking dish. Pour the wine over the fish. Bake about 40 minutes, until the flesh is fork-tender. Remove to a warm platter and keep warm. Stir the drippings with a fork and add the sour cream. Heat the mixture over medium-low heat. Spoon over the fish and serve.

Kobarid Spicy Fish

4 servings

On the Soca River in one of the most beautiful and peaceful spots in Slovenia, Kobarid was immortalized by Ernest Hemingway in his novel, A Farewell to Arms, *although he refers to the place by its Italian name, Caporetto. Restaurants in the area specialize in seafood such as this typical dish and also fish kebabs.*

¼ cup olive oil

1 large yellow onion, peeled and minced

1 to 2 tablespoons paprika

1½ pounds white fish, sliced into 8 (¼-inch) slices

1 tablespoon tomato paste

1 tablespoon fresh lemon juice

2 garlic cloves, crushed

1 bay leaf

Salt and freshly ground pepper

In a large skillet heat the oil over medium-high heat. Add the onion and sauté for 3 minutes. Stir in the paprika and cook 1 minute. Add the fish and brown on both sides, adding more oil, if needed. Stir in the tomato paste, lemon juice, and ¼ cup water and cook for 2 to 3 minutes. Add the garlic and bay leaf, and season with salt and pepper. Reduce the heat to medium-low. Cook, covered, about 10 minutes, until the fish is tender.

Fish Kebabs

In Slovenia fish kebabs are commonly cooked over outdoor open fires.
They are popular street snacks and served at everyday and company meals.
They can be broiled indoors as well.

---

2 pounds firm-fleshed fish (halibut or salmon)

1 medium yellow onion, finely chopped

¼ cup fresh lemon juice

¾ cup olive oil

¼ teaspoon crumbled dried oregano

Salt and freshly ground pepper

Onion slices

Bay leaves

Preheat the broiler.

Remove and discard any skin from the fish. Cut into 1-inch cubes. In a large bowl combine the fish with the chopped onion, lemon juice, oil, and oregano, and season with salt and pepper. Leave to marinate in the refrigerator, mixing occasionally, for 1 hour. Thread the fish on skewers, alternating with onion slices and bay leaves. Arrange the skewers on a piece of foil set on a baking sheet. Cover with the remaining marinade. Broil for about 15 minutes, or until fish is tender, turning once or twice. Serve the kebabs on the skewers.

Italian Tuna Fish

4 to 6 servings

This typical dish is made with fresh tuna steaks and a piquant sauce flavored with anchovies, herbs, tomatoes, and lemon juice.

2 tablespoons olive oil

1 large yellow onion, peeled and finely chopped

1 garlic clove, crushed

3 large tomatoes, peeled and chopped

1 cup tomato juice

1 tablespoon fresh lemon juice

4 flat anchovies, chopped

½ teaspoon dried oregano or basil

Salt and freshly ground pepper

2 pounds tuna steaks, cut into 4 to 6 pieces

In a large skillet heat the oil over medium-high heat. Add the onion and garlic and sauté for 4 minutes. Add the tomatoes and cook, stirring occasionally, 4 minutes. Add the tomato juice, lemon juice, anchovies, and oregano. Season with salt and pepper. Reduce the heat to medium-low and cook, uncovered, 15 minutes. Add the tuna to the sauce. Continue cooking, covered, about 15 minutes, until tender, the exact time depends on the thickness of the steaks. Serve with the sauce spooned over the steaks.

Cuisines of the Alps

Baked Fish with Sour Cream

As a landlocked country, Austria's primary sources of fish are the Danube River and Alpine lakes and streams that supply a good amount of three favorites – trout, carp, and pike. The latter, called hecht, *is very often baked with sour cream. A small restaurant on a mountainside overlooking Innsbruck, the Tirolean capital, has an exhilarating view and the inviting fare. It is a marvelous place to enjoy a dish similar to this one.*

---

2 pounds pike or whitefish, cleaned

3 tablespoons unsalted butter

2 medium yellow onions, peeled and sliced

2 cups sour cream, at room temperature

2 tablespoons capers, drained

2 tablespoons minced fresh dill or parsley

Salt and freshly ground pepper

1 lemon, sliced

Paprika

Preheat the oven to 350 degrees. Grease a shallow baking dish.

Leave the fish whole or cut them into 4 to 6 pieces. Place in the prepared baking dish. In a small skillet melt the butter over medium-high heat. Add the onions and sauté for 5 minutes. Add the sour cream, capers, and dill. Season with salt and pepper. Mix well and spoon the sour cream mixture over the fish. Top with lemon slices and sprinkle with paprika. Bake, basting occasionally with the drippings, about 20 minutes, until the fish is fork-tender.

Verbier Fried Salmon

4 servings

High on a Valais plateau above the Val de Bagnes with the 9,915-foot Mont Gele towering behind, Verbier is a famous ski resort with the largest aerial cableway in Europe and a summer sports center. Although its sophisticated and old-style restaurants offer a number of notable cheese specialties, this traditional salmon dish is usually on the menu.

2 pounds salmon, cut into 1-inch slices

3 tablespoons fresh lemon juice

Salt and freshly ground pepper

¾ cup all-purpose flour

½ cup unsalted butter

3 tablespoons olive or vegetable oil

2 medium yellow onions, peeled and thinly sliced

3 tablespoons finely chopped fresh dill or parsley

1 lemon, sliced

Place the salmon in a shallow dish and sprinkle with the lemon juice, salt, and pepper. Let stand 30 minutes. Pat the salmon dry and dip it in the flour. In a large skillet melt the butter over medium-high heat. Add salmon, turning once, about 7 minutes total, until golden brown on both sides.

Meanwhile, heat the oil in a small skillet over medium-high heat. Add the onion and sauté it for 5 minutes. Place the salmon on a serving platter. Top with the fried onions and sprinkle with dill. Serve garnished with lemon slices.

German Pike with Sauerkraut

This flavorful German baked fish is made with three favorite German foods – pike, sauerkraut, and sour cream. Have your fishmonger skin and bone the pike and cut it into 2-inch fillets. Take home the trimmings and bones as well as the fillets.

---

2 pounds pike or any white firm-fleshed fish

2 medium yellow onions, peeled and chopped

1 large carrot, peeled and sliced

Salt and freshly ground pepper

3 to 4 tablespoons unsalted butter

2 tablespoons all-purpose flour

2 tablespoons chopped fresh dill or parsley

1/2 cup sour cream, at room temperature

2 pounds (4 cups) sauerkraut, drained

Fine dry bread crumbs

Preheat the oven to 375 degrees. Grease a shallow baking dish.

In a large saucepan over medium-high heat prepare a court bouillon by combining the pike trimmings and bones, 1 chopped onion, the carrot, 4 cups water, salt, and pepper, Bring to a boil, then reduce the heat to medium-low. Cook, covered, 30 minutes. Strain, reserving the liquid.

In a large saucepan melt 3 tablespoons of the butter over medium-high heat. Add the remaining chopped onion and sauté for 4 minutes. Stir in the flour and cook, stirring, for 2 minutes. Add the strained court bouillon, a little at a time. Cook slowly, stirring, until the mixture is thickened and smooth. Add the dill and sour cream. Heat the sauce just long enough to heat through.

Spoon a layer of sauerkraut into the prepared baking dish. Top with half the fish fillets and half the sauce. Sprinkle with half the bread crumbs. Repeat layers, topping with bread crumbs. Dot with the remaining 1 tablespoon butter and bake for about 30 minutes, until the fish is tender and the top is golden.

Austrian Fish Goulash

The Austrians borrowed a well-flavored fish stew, or goulash, from their neighbors, the Hungarians. In Austria an assortment of freshwater fish is used to make the dish.

---

2 pounds white fish fillets

Salt and freshly ground pepper

2 tablespoons unsalted butter

2 tablespoons vegetable oil

2 large yellow onions, peeled and thinly sliced

1 garlic clove, minced

1 to 2 tablespoons paprika

2 large tomatoes, peeled and chopped

6 medium potatoes, peeled and diced

Cut the fish into cubes. Season with salt and pepper and set aside.

In a large saucepan melt the butter with the oil over medium-high heat. Add the onions and garlic and sauté for 4 minutes. Stir in the paprika and cook for 1 minute. Add the tomatoes and cook 4 minutes. Add potatoes and water to cover. Cook, covered, for 10 minutes. Add the fish and cook until tender, about 10 minutes. Do not stir while mixture is cooking but occasionally shake the pan if the ingredients stick to the bottom. Add a little more water while cooking, if needed.

Tuna with Tomato Sauce

*This easy-to-prepare Italian dish may be made with fresh tuna steaks or canned tuna.
It's good for an informal luncheon or supper after a day of mountain climbing.*

---

2 tablespoons olive oil

1 medium yellow
  onion, peeled and
  chopped

1 garlic clove, crushed

3 tablespoons tomato
  paste

1½ cups dry white
  wine

½ teaspoon dried
  thyme or basil

Salt and freshly
  ground pepper

2 tablespoons
  chopped fresh
  parsley

4 fresh tuna steaks,
  sautéed and kept
  warm

In a medium saucepan heat the oil over medium-high
heat. Add the onion and garlic and sauté 4 minutes. Add
the tomato paste, white wine, and thyme. Season with salt
and pepper and mix well. Reduce the heat to medium-low
and cook, uncovered, 10 minutes. Add the parsley and
serve the sauce over the fried tuna steaks.

Sautéed Scampi

Scampi is one of the great gastronomic treats in northern Italy and Switzerland. Sweet and tender, they are something like shrimp but are distinctive and are found only in the deep waters of the Adriatic Sea.

¼ cup olive oil

2 garlic cloves, crushed or minced

½ cup minced scallions, with some tops

2 pounds shelled and cleaned raw large shrimp

1 tablespoon capers, drained

½ cup finely chopped fresh parsley

Salt and freshly ground pepper

In a large skillet heat the oil over medium-high heat. Add the garlic and scallions and sauté for 3 minutes. Add the shrimp and sauté until they become pink, a few minutes. Stir in the capers and parsley and season with salt and pepper. Reduce the heat to medium-low and cook 5 minutes. Serve at once.

Piran Baked Fish with Vegetables

4 to 6 servings

Picturesque Piran, sitting at the tip of a narrow peninsula on the Slovenian coastline, was settled by the Romans and built in the Venetian style. Protected as a cultural monument, Piran is the best preserved historic town on the Adriatic Sea. This typical fish dish is served in local restaurants.

---

2 pounds white fish fillets (carp, pike, perch, or flounder)

½ cup olive oil

2 medium yellow onions, peeled and sliced

2 garlic cloves, crushed

2 leeks, white parts only, cleaned and sliced

½ cup peeled and diced carrots

½ cup thinly sliced green beans

3 medium tomatoes, peeled and chopped

3 tablespoons chopped fresh dill

⅓ cup chopped fresh parsley

¼ cup raisins

2 tablespoons fresh lemon juice

Salt and freshly ground pepper

Preheat the oven to 350 degrees. Grease a shallow baking dish.

Arrange the fish in the prepared baking dish. In a medium skillet heat the oil over medium-high heat. Add the onions, garlic, and leeks and sauté for 4 minutes. Add the carrots, green beans, and tomatoes and sauté for 5 minutes. Stir in the dill, parsley, raisins, and lemon juice and season with salt and pepper. Mix well. Spoon over the fish fillets, spreading evenly. Bake, covered, about 25 minutes, until fish is tender.

Meat, Poultry, and Game

Among the gastronomic delights that grace Alpine tables, meats are the most treasured and are very often the stars of family and company repasts. The diverse selection of excellent and innovative national favorites made with pork, veal, lamb, beef, and variety meats is particularly noteworthy for its endless appeal to all tastes. Meat in one form or another is the cornerstone of each country's cookery.

Since the beginning of time man has been preoccupied with obtaining meat for his daily meals. At first he was limited to the hunting of wild animals, but with the birth of civilization the flesh of domesticated cows, pigs, and sheep also became available.

For centuries, however, the term meat was applied to any number of foods including fish, poultry, vegetables, and nuts, as well as to the flesh of animals. In modern times we have adopted the practice of using the term primarily for the flesh of our domesticated animals. That of wild animals is called game.

Over the years the most favored meat in Alpine countries has been pork. Since everything but "the oink" is edible and can be made into one creation or another, pork very often provided the main meat supply in a large part of the mountain lands. Every small town still has one or more shop well stocked with ample supplies of fresh and cured pork and great, interesting pork dishes are found in all the Alpine cuisines.

Throughout the Alpine region there are also great beef dishes, including thick rich stews, meatballs, and meat loaf variations, which utilize cuts other than roasts and steaks. A particular specialty in Austria is boiled beef. Despite the popularity of beef, veal is much preferred in Alpine nations. It is always a superlative treat, made into imaginative creations. Lamb is also important in most regions.

The people of the Alpine countries have long been ardent devotees of their great variety of poultry and game birds, which still accord places of honor on their dining tables. Fanciers of chicken, duck, goose, pheasant, partridge, or woodcock, to name only a few, can discover a great many innovative dishes. Both domesticated and wild species are deeply respected and sought-after fare throughout the Alps.

Fondue Bourguignonne

One of Switzerland's best known meat dishes is a fondue made with small cubes of beef cooked in oil and then dipped in various sauces. It is a popular supper dish in Alpine resorts where guests enjoy cooking it themselves at the table.

A fondue pot or similar utensil, long-handled forks, dinner plates, and small bowls for the sauces are necessary for cooking. Traditional accompaniments are thinly sliced deep-fried potatoes or baked potatoes and a green salad. The Swiss typically enjoy a dry red wine with the fondue. Although any good beef may be used, a tender cut such as sirloin is preferable. A few sauce recipes are included below but prepared sauces may be used, if desired. These might include tartar or chili sauce or Russian dressing.

---

3 pounds boneless beef tenderloin, sirloin, or other cut of beef

Peanut oil

Assorted sauces (recipes follow)

Cut off any fat from the beef, discard it, and cut the beef into 1-inch cubes. Pile the beef on a platter or wooden board. Before cooking the meat, have the table set with an empty plate, long-handled fork, dinner fork (and other necessary implements if other foods are included) for each person.

Heat 1½ to 2 inches of oil in the fondue pot. To cook the meat, each person spears a cube of meat with a long-handled fork and cooks it in the hot oil to the desired degree of doneness. The meat is then dipped in one or more of the sauces, removed from the long-handled fork onto the plate, and eaten with a dinner fork. Continue cooking until all the meat is used.

Mustard Sauce

1 cup sour cream

2 tablespoons mustard

2 teaspoons prepared
horseradish

Salt and freshly
ground pepper

Combine the sour cream, mustard, and horseradish. Season with salt and pepper.

Tartar Sauce

1 cup mayonnaise

¼ cup chopped sweet
pickle

3 tablespoons
chopped scallions

1 tablespoon finely
chopped fresh
parsley

I teaspoon mustard

Salt and freshly
ground pepper

Combine the mayonnaise, pickle, scallions, parsley, and mustard. Season with salt and pepper.

Russian Dressing

1 cup mayonnaise

½ cup chili sauce

3 tablespoons pickle
relish

Salt and freshly
ground pepper

Combine the mayonnaise, chili sauce, and pickle relish. Season with salt and pepper.

Swiss Berner Platte

6 to 8 servings

This Swiss specialty made with sauerkraut and a variety of meats including several sausages and sometimes pigs' ears, feet, and tongue, is called berner platte, *named for the attractive capital, Bern. Once a typical farmer's dish, it's now prepared for home meals and parties.*

---

6 medium waxy potatoes

2 pounds sauerkraut

2 tablespoons bacon or pork fat

2 medium yellow onions, peeled and chopped

8 whole peppercorns

10 juniper berries

2½ cups dry white wine

½ pound bacon in one piece

6 smoked pork chops

1 pound pork sausage links, cooked and drained

6 bratwurst or knockwurst, braised and drained

6 thick slices cooked ham

3 cups green beans

3 tablespoons unsalted butter

1 garlic clove, minced

Salt and freshly ground pepper

Put the potatoes in a pot with water to cover. Bring to a boil and cook until tender. When cooked, drain, peel, and keep warm in a serving bowl.

Meanwhile, rinse the sauerkraut and drain well. In a pot heat the fat over medium-high heat. Add the onions and sauté for 4 minutes. Add the sauerkraut and sauté, mixing with a fork, for 5 minutes. Add the peppercorns, juniper berries, wine, and bacon. Reduce the heat to medium-low. Add the pork chops, sausages, bratwurst, and ham. Continue cooking until all the ingredients are done, about 30 minutes.

While the meat is cooking, put the beans in a pot with water to cover. When tender, drain. Put in a bowl with the butter and garlic, and season with salt and pepper. Keep warm.

When the meat is cooked, remove and discard the peppercorns and juniper berries To serve, spoon sauerkraut onto a platter. Surround with the meats. Serve the potatoes and green beans as accompaniments.

Vitello Tonnato

This excellent cold Italian dish is superb for summer entertaining. It is traditionally made with tender milk-fed veal, vitello, *and a rich tuna sauce.*

---

1 boneless veal roast,
  3 to 3½ pounds,
  tied securely

4 flat anchovy fillets,
  chopped

4 whole cloves

1 medium onion

2 medium celery
  stalks, chopped

2 medium carrots,
  peeled and chopped

2 medium bay leaves

5 parsley sprigs

8 whole peppercorns

Salt

Tuna Sauce (recipe
  follows)

Garnishes (optional):
  drained capers,
  finely chopped
  fresh parsley,
  lemon slices

With the point of a sharp knife make several small slits in the veal. Insert the anchovy pieces into the slits. Place the roast in a pot. Stick the cloves in the onion and add to the pot along with the celery, carrots, bay leaves, parsley, peppercorns, and salt (only a little because the anchovies add saltiness). Pour in enough water to cover and bring to a boil over medium-high heat. Reduce the heat to medium-low and cook, covered, about 1½ hours, until the meat is tender. Carefully remove the meat from the pot and cool. Discard cooking liquid.

Meanwhile, prepare the Tuna Sauce. When the meat is cool, cut it into thin slices and arrange attractively on a platter. Spoon the Tuna Sauce over the meat. Refrigerate 2 or 3 hours or until ready to serve. Serve with garnishes, if desired.

Tuna Sauce

Combine tuna, anchovies, oil, lemon juice, capers, parsley, and pepper in a blender. Purée to make a smooth and fairly liquid sauce.

2 (6-ounce) cans tuna,
  drained

6 flat anchovy fillets,
  diced

1 cup olive oil

Juice of 2 medium
  lemons

2 tablespoons drained
  capers

2 tablespoons chopped
  fresh parsley

Freshly ground pepper

French Pork Roast

8 to 10 servings

This pork roast is traditionally made with fresh sage leaves that are inserted into the meat several hours before cooking. Use fresh sage, if available, but the meat will be flavorful with only thyme and bay leaves.

---

1 boneless roast loin of pork, 7 to 8 pounds

4 garlic cloves, cut into slivers

Fresh sage leaves (optional)

2 teaspoons dried thyme

2 medium bay leaves, crumbled

Salt and freshly ground pepper

3 to 4 tablespoons olive oil

½ cup dry white wine

½ cup chopped fresh parsley

Trim any excess fat from roast. With the point of a sharp knife make small incisions in the flesh and insert the garlic slivers and sage (if using) into them. Rub the pork with the thyme, bay leaves, salt, and pepper. Put in a large bowl and sprinkle with oil and wine. Refrigerate, covered for 4 to 5 hours.

Preheat the oven to 325 degrees. Arrange the pork loin on a rack in a shallow roasting pan. Pour any liquid over the pork. Roast, uncovered, for 4 to 5 hours, allowing 35 to 40 minutes per pound. When cooked, sprinkle the parsley over the roast.

Osso Buco

This traditional dish from the northern Italian city of Milan is a favorite dinner specialty in the country's Alpine regions. The name means "hollow bones" and one of the best aspects of the dish is the marrow of the bones, which is extracted and eaten. After the meat has been cooked they are sprinkled with gremolata, *an essential part of the dish made with a combination of chopped garlic, parsley, and grated lemon peel. Osso buco is traditionally served with a large dish of rice, usually a Milanese risotto.*

---

7 to 8 pounds veal shank or shin with marrow, cut into 2 ($\frac{1}{2}$-inch) pieces

Salt and freshly ground pepper

All-purpose flour

About $\frac{1}{3}$ cup unsalted butter or olive oil

1 cup chopped yellow onions

2 garlic cloves, crushed

1 cup dry white wine

3 cups canned Italian plum tomatoes, drained and chopped

1 cup beef broth or bouillon

1 bouquet garni (parsley, thyme, bay leaf)

1 tablespoon grated lemon peel

3 tablespoons chopped fresh parsley

Wipe the veal pieces dry. Sprinkle with salt and pepper and a little flour. In a heavy casserole melt the butter or heat the oil over medium-high heat. Add the veal a few pieces at a time and brown on both sides, then transfer to a platter. Sauté the onions and 1 garlic clove in the drippings, adding more butter if needed, for 4 minutes. Arrange the veal to stand upright over the onions. Pour wine over them and spoon the tomatoes on top. Add the stock and the bouquet garni. Bring the mixture to a boil, then reduce the heat to medium-low. Cook, covered, for $1\frac{1}{2}$ to 2 hours, until meat is tender. Remove and discard bouquet garni. Combine the remaining clove of garlic, lemon peel, and parsley and sprinkle over the meat.

Bavarian Rouladen

Braised stuffed beef rolls, rouladen, *are one of the great Bavarian favorites for a midday meal. They are traditionally served with red cabbage and dumplings or potatoes, accompanied by a stein of beer. In Germany, thinly sliced beef, specially prepared for* rouladen, *is sold at most meat markets. In America, round steak is a good substitute, but it should be sliced thinly and pounded with a mallet.*

---

2 pounds round steak, trimmed of fat

Dijon mustard

4 slices thin bacon, diced

3 tablespoons minced dill pickle or relish

1 large yellow onion, peeled and finely chopped

All-purpose flour

3 tablespoons unsalted butter

2 cups beef bouillon

Salt and freshly ground pepper

3 tablespoons finely chopped fresh parsley

Cut the meat into 4 thin rectangles, about 4 inches wide and 8 inches long. Pound each piece with a mallet to make it as thin as possible. Arrange the beef on a flat surface and spread the top side of each piece with mustard. In a small dish combine the bacon, pickle, and onion. Place a large spoonful of the mixture on each slice of meat. Roll up carefully and secure with toothpicks, making sure that the filling is completely enclosed. Dredge each roll with flour.

In a large skillet melt the butter over medium-high heat. Add the *rouladen* and brown on both sides. Add the bouillon and season with salt and pepper. Reduce the heat to medium-low and cook slowly, covered, about 1 hour, until the meat is tender. Stir in the parsley. Serve at once.

Veal Birds

*These small stuffed packets of veal are sometimes called "poor men's birds,"
as they were once served as a substitute for small roasted birds. They are, however,
not poor fare but elegant and inviting creations.*

---

8 thin veal scallops

8 slices prosciutto or
other thinly cut
cured ham

8 slices mozzarella
cheese

⅓ cup unsalted butter

Salt and freshly
ground pepper

⅓ cup Marsala wine

⅓ cup chopped fresh
parsley

With a wooden mallet flatten the veal scallops, making them as thin as possible but being careful not to tear the meat. Arrange a slice of prosciutto and mozzarella on each piece of veal. Fold to enclose the prosciutto and cheese in the veal and fasten with toothpicks. In a large skillet melt the butter over medium-high heat. Add the veal birds and cook until tender and brown on all sides. Season with salt and pepper. Remove to a warm plate. Add the Marsala to the drippings, heat and pour over the birds. Sprinkle with parsley.

Slovenian Skewered Meatballs

6 servings

These Slovenian skewered meatballs are commonly sold throughout the country at sidewalk stalls or small open-air restaurants from where their captivating aroma permeates city and village streets. The meatballs are eaten as snacks, appetizers, or entrées.

1½ pounds ground
   lean pork
1½ pounds ground
   lean veal or beef
Salt and freshly
   ground pepper

In a large mixing bowl, combine the pork and veal. Season with salt and pepper. Shape into small sausage forms and thread on a skewer. Cook the meatballs over charcoal or under a heated broiler, turning once, until the meat is cooked. Serve with fried onions.

Austrian Wiener Schnitzel

Austrians are very fond of schnitzels, thin breaded cutlets of meat, usually veal. The most popular kind is a specialty of Vienna, a fried breaded veal cutlet enjoyed throughout the country as a favorite dinner entrée.

---

4 large veal cutlets,
(1½ to 2 pounds
total)
All-purpose flour
Salt and freshly
ground pepper
2 eggs, lightly beaten
Fine dry bread crumbs
Lard and vegetable oil
for frying
4 lemon wedges

Fill three bowls with the following: flour seasoned with salt and pepper, the beaten eggs, and the bread crumbs. Neatly trim each veal cutlet of fat and make slits slantwise along the edges. Pound well with a wooden mallet, being careful not to tear the flesh. Dip each cutlet first in flour, shaking off any extra. Then in the beaten egg and lastly in the bread crumbs. Again shake off any extra.

In a large skillet over medium-high heat add equal proportions of lard and oil to make ½ inch liquid. When hot, add the cutlets and fry, 1 or 2 at a time, until golden brown on both sides. Add more lard and oil as needed. Serve at once garnished with lemon wedges.

Beef Daube

6 to 8 servings

In the French Alps there are several marvelous dishes, made with meat, poultry, or game, cooked slowly into flavorful stews. Traditionally each is cooked in a daubiere, a special earthenware pot, and the finished dish is called daube.

---

3 pounds stewing beef, cubed and trimmed of fat

1 cup dry white or red wine

¼ cup brandy (optional)

¼ cup plus 2 table-spoons olive oil

2 large yellow onions, peeled and thinly sliced

4 medium carrots, peeled and diced

2 medium bay leaves

1 teaspoon dried thyme

½ cup finely chopped fresh parsley

Salt and freshly ground pepper

½ cup diced thick bacon

2 garlic cloves, crushed

3 medium tomatoes, peeled and chopped

1 cup sliced fresh mushrooms

1 strip orange peel

½ teaspoon dried rosemary

12 black olives, pitted

In a large bowl combine the beef, wine, brandy, ¼ cup of the olive oil, 1 sliced onion, 2 diced carrots, the bay leaves, thyme, and 2 tablespoons of the parsley. Season with salt and pepper and marinate in refrigerator for 2 to 3 hours, stirring occasionally.

When ready to cook, put the bacon, garlic, remaining 2 tablespoons oil, 1 sliced onion, and 2 diced carrots in a pot over medium-high heat and sauté for 5 minutes. Remove the meat from the marinade, reserving the marinade, and wipe the meat dry. Brown a few pieces of meat at a time in the heated oil, pushing the vegetables aside. When all the meat is browned, mix in the tomatoes, mushrooms, orange peel, and rosemary and season with salt and pepper. Pour in the reserved marinade, including the vegetables. Reduce the heat to medium-low and cook, covered, for 30 minutes. Stir in the olives and cook for another 30 minutes. Then, add the remaining 6 tablespoons parsley. Remove and discard the bay leaves.

Ham-Noodle Casserole

4 servings

*A common dish in Alpine regions is this casserole made with noodles and ham.
It may be prepared beforehand and served as a weekend luncheon or supper entrée
after a day spent outdoors.*

Fine dry bread crumbs

1/2 pound wide egg
  noodles, broken

3 tablespoons unsalted
  butter

2 eggs, separated

1 cup light cream

1 cup finely chopped
  cooked ham

2 tablespoons minced
  fresh dill or parsley

Salt and freshly
  ground pepper

Preheat the oven to 350 degrees. Grease a 1½-quart casserole and sprinkle the inside with bread crumbs.

Cook the noodles in boiling salted water over medium-high heat until tender; drain. In a large saucepan melt the butter over medium-low heat. Add the noodles and sauté until golden. In a small bowl combine the egg yolks and cream. Add to the noodles. Mix in the ham and dill and season with salt and pepper. Beat the egg whites until stiff and fold into the noodle mixture. Put in the prepared dish. Bake about 35 minutes, until cooked. Serve at once.

Bratwurst in Beer

4 servings

Bratwurst, small pork sausages, originated in Nuremberg. They are popular in Bavaria and featured in almost all of the local restaurants. Grilled over a beech wood fire, and served with peppery sauerkraut and fresh horseradish, bratwurst are always a welcome repast. One of the places they taste best is Nuremberg's annual Christkindlesmarkt *("Christ Child's market"), held during the cold December days and evenings where they are served on crusty rolls with sharp mustard. The* Markt *is permeated with their tantalizing aroma, as well as that of other native fare sold to hungry visitors.*

---

12 bratwurst

1 tablespoon unsalted butter

2 medium yellow onions, chopped

1 cup beer

Salt and freshly ground pepper

1 tablespoon all-purpose flour

2 tablespoons chopped fresh parsley

Put the bratwurst in a medium saucepan. Cover with boiling water and cook over medium-high heat for 3 minutes. Drain.

In a large skillet melt butter over medium-high heat. Add the bratwurst and brown on all sides. Remove to a warm plate and pour off all except 2 tablespoons of fat. Add the onions and sauté for 4 minutes. Return the sausages to the skillet and add the beer. Season with salt and pepper and reduce the heat to medium-low. Cook, covered, for 15 minutes. Remove bratwurst to a warm platter.

In a small bowl mix the flour with a little water. Stir the flour mixture into the hot liquid in the skillet. Cook, stirring, until it forms a thick sauce. Add the parsley and pour the sauce over the bratwurst. Serve with mashed potatoes.

Tyrolean Goulash

Hungary's national dish, gulyás, *meaning shepherd's or herdsmen's stew, is eaten in one form or another in several Alpine countries. It is thought that* gulyás *was created by shepherds, who cooked it on an outdoor fire. Traditionally, it is prepared in a large pot called* bogracs. *Today there are many versions but generally the stew is thick and made with beef, onions, and paprika. It is thickened, not with flour, but by long, slow cooking.*

2 pounds boneless beef chuck or stew meat

2 tablespoons lard or other fat

2 large yellow onions, peeled and chopped

2 to 3 tablespoons paprika

Salt and freshly ground pepper

3 medium tomatoes, peeled and chopped

1 pound potatoes, peeled and diced

Wipe the meat dry. In a pot heat the lard over medium-high heat. Add the meat and brown on all sides. Push the meat aside and add the onions and more lard, if needed. Sauté 3 to 4 minutes, stir in the paprika, and cook 1 minute. Season with salt and pepper. Add enough water to cover ingredients. Reduce the heat to medium-low and cook slowly, covered, for 1 hour. Add the tomatoes and potatoes; continue cooking another 30 minutes, until the beef and potatoes are tender. During the cooking add a little more water, if needed, but the final gravy should be thick.

Poulet Marengo

In 1800, after Napoleon defeated the Austrians at Marengo in Italy's Piedmont region, he asked his chef to create a special dish to celebrate. Since they were away from the supply wagons, he had to hunt for provisions in the ravaged countryside. According to the story, his scouts found a scrawny chicken, three eggs, four tomatoes, six crayfish, and some seasonings. Napoleon was delighted with the chef's creation. Mushrooms and wine were later additions.

2 frying chickens, (about 2½ pounds each), cut up

Salt and freshly ground pepper

¼ cup, plus 2 tablespoons olive oil

3 tablespoons unsalted butter

1 pound medium-size mushrooms, cleaned

2 garlic cloves

1 cup chopped yellow onions

⅓ cup tomato purée

1 cup dry white wine

4 medium tomatoes, peeled, seeded, and chopped

1 bouquet garni (bay leaf, parsley, thyme)

Garnishes:

8 eggs, deep fried in olive oil

4 slices French bread, fried in oil and cut into triangles

16 large shrimp cooked, shelled, and deveined

Wash the chicken and pat it dry. Season with salt and pepper. In a large heavy casserole heat the oil and butter over medium-high heat. Add the chicken and fry on all sides until golden brown. Remove to a warm platter.

Carefully pull the stems off half the mushrooms. Reserve the caps. Slice the stems and the remaining ½ pound mushrooms. Sauté the mushrooms in the drippings for 4 minutes. With a slotted spoon, remove to a plate. Add the garlic and onions to the drippings and sauté for 4 minutes. Stir in the tomato purée and wine. Bring to a boil and cook over high heat 5 minutes. Return the chicken to the casserole. Add the tomatoes and the bouquet garni. Season with salt and pepper. Reduce the heat to medium-low and cook, covered, 35 minutes, until the chicken is tender. Add the reserved sautéed mushroom slices and mushroom caps 10 minutes before cooking is finished.

When chicken is done, remove and discard bouquet garni. To serve, arrange the chicken pieces on a large platter. Spoon the sauce, including the sliced mushrooms, over the chicken. Arrange the fried eggs, each on a toast triangle, and shrimp around the chicken.

Chicken Cacciatora

This "hunter's style" chicken, a flavorful and attractive creation cooked in a colorful sauce made of a medley of ingredients, is favorite fare in the Italian Alps.

1 frying chicken (about 3 pounds), cut up

Salt and freshly ground pepper

3 tablespoons olive oil

2 tablespoons unsalted butter

2 medium onions, peeled and sliced

1 or 2 garlic cloves, crushed

4 medium tomatoes, peeled, seeded, and chopped

1 can (8 ounces) tomato sauce

½ cup dry white wine

2 tablespoons chopped fresh parsley

½ teaspoon dried basil

Wash the chicken and pat dry. Season with salt and pepper. In a large skillet heat the oil and butter over medium-high heat. Add chicken and brown on all sides, turning once or twice. Remove from the pan and keep warm. Add the onions and garlic to the pan and sauté for 5 minutes. Add the tomatoes, tomato sauce, wine, parsley, and basil. Season with salt and pepper and cook slowly, uncovered, 10 minutes. Return the chicken pieces to the skillet. Reduce the heat to medium-low. Cook, covered, about 35 minutes, until the chicken is tender.

Poulet en Cocotte

6 servings

One of the best French and Swiss methods of preparing poultry is to cook it in a tightly sealed casserole on top of the stove or in the oven, as the flavor is enhanced by the slow steaming process. This is an excellent one-dish meal.

¼ cup mustard

1 tablespoon horseradish

2 teaspoons mixed dried herbs

Salt

2 broiler-fryer chickens, cut up

¼ cup unsalted butter

¾ cup chicken broth

¾ cup dry white wine

4 teaspoons all-purpose flour

Preheat the oven to 500 degrees.

Mix the mustard, horseradish, herbs, and salt. Rub the chicken pieces with the mixture.

In a heavy ovenproof pot melt butter over medium-high heat. Add the chicken and brown it in the oven, 15 minutes on each side. Reduce the heat to 350 degrees. Add the broth and wine. Bake, covered, 30 minutes longer, until the chicken is tender. Remove the chicken to a platter. Add the flour to the pan juices and cook on the stove, stirring constantly, to make a thick gravy. Pour over the chicken.

Braised Duck with Red Cabbage

Two characteristic and superb German foods, duck and red cabbage, are combined in this specialty to make one of the country's best dishes.

---

1 duckling (about 5 pounds), cut up

Salt and freshly ground pepper

1 medium head red cabbage

$\frac{1}{3}$ cup lemon juice

$\frac{1}{4}$ pound salt pork, diced (optional)

1 large yellow onion, peeled and chopped

1 tablespoon all-purpose flour

About $\frac{1}{2}$ cup red wine

1 teaspoon sugar

Preheat the oven to 375 degrees.

Wash the duckling and pat dry. Season with salt and pepper. Place in a shallow baking pan and roast for 30 minutes.

Meanwhile, blanch the cabbage in a large saucepan in boiling salted water over medium-high heat for 5 minutes. Drain. Remove the core and any wilted leaves. Sprinkle with lemon juice and shred.

In a large saucepan fry the salt pork over medium-high heat for 5 minutes. Add the onion and sauté for 5 minutes. Mix in the flour. Add the cabbage, red wine, and sugar. Season with salt and pepper. Reduce the heat to medium-low and cook, covered, 30 minutes. Put the partially cooked duck and some of the pan drippings over the cabbage. Continue to cook slowly, covered, for 1 hour, or until the duck is cooked, adding more red wine during the cooking, if needed.

German Roast Goose

Flavorful roast goose is popular fare in several Alpine countries, traditionally served on certain holidays, particularly Christmas. Although some common stuffings are made with fruits, this one containing sauerkraut is more typical of the Alps.

---

1 fresh or frozen
ready-to-cook goose,
8 to 10 pounds

Salt and freshly
ground pepper

Juice of 1 lemon

1 large yellow onion,
peeled and finely
chopped

2 pounds sauerkraut,
drained

½ teaspoon crushed
juniper berries or
caraway seeds

½ cup dry white wine

Preheat the oven to 325 degrees.

Wash the goose and pat dry. Remove any fat from the cavity and reserve. Rub inside and out with salt and pepper. Prick the skin in several places and rub with lemon juice. In a large saucepan, melt 2 tablespoons of goose fat over medium-high heat. Add the onion and sauté for 4 minutes. Add the sauerkraut and sauté for 2 to 3 minutes. Add the juniper berries and wine. Season with salt and pepper. Bring to a boil and remove from the heat. Stuff the sauerkraut mixture lightly into the goose. Close the cavity by sewing or with poultry pins. Place in a roasting pan and roast, uncovered, for 3 hours, or until tender. Spoon off any fat as it accumulates in the pan. If any of the stuffing is left over, heat and serve with the goose.

Vegetables and Salads

Perfectly prepared vegetables, available in exceptional variety, and superb salads are Alpine gastronomic delights. Each country has an enviable number of delectable and interesting vegetable dishes. Alpine cooks have long been experts in making the gifts of the garden into inviting creations that enhance the pleasure of dining.

A fascinating aspect of Alpine vegetable cookery is the wondrous ways that both familiar and unfamiliar vegetables are prepared. Over the years, a great deal of attention has been paid to their growth, cooking method, seasoning, and presentation. In some instances even their proper culinary companions have been divined. The French, as one example, have long understood that turnips and duckling, beans and lamb, and spinach and ham belong together.

No matter how humble, each vegetable grown in the Alpine regions became an important part of one or more of the cuisines. Thus, cooks are as well acquainted with the preparation of salsify, fennel, celery root, and sorrel, as they are with peas, carrots, beets, and beans. To understand the versatility and goodness of vegetable cookery, we can look to one of the oldest and best known vegetable "families," the onion. All of the members, chives, garlic, leeks, scallions, shallots, and onion varieties – white, red, and yellow – are highly esteemed throughout the regions of the Alps.

Switzerland's picturesque capital of Bern, a handsome preserved medieval city, sets aside a special day to honor the humble onion. Annually, on November 22, thousands of Swiss and foreign visitors gather at a colorful Onion Market to enjoy an unusual autumn harvest holiday alive with merrymaking and good eating.

When traveling in Alpine towns and villages it is always a delight to see the colorful displays of fresh vegetables, attractively arranged, in open-air markets, sidewalk stalls, and groceries. Root and tuber, seed and pod, stem and flower, and leafy vegetables are a delight to behold. Although canned and frozen vegetables are available, cooks prefer the fresh varieties and in most regions they are eaten in season, enjoyed while garden-fresh and tender.

The recipes included here are for dishes featuring vegetables that can be served as accompaniments to other foods or, in some cases, as entrées. Generally speaking, salads in Alpine countries are enjoyed either as an appetizer or with the main course. Although salads feature vegetables as their most popular ingredients, some are made with fruit.

Italian Broiled Tomatoes

12 servings

Actually a fruit, the tomato is one of the most popular and versatile Italian foods, and is traditionally prepared and served as a vegetable. Tomatoes are a good source of nutrient minerals as they contain calcium and iron. They are also rich in vitamin C.

---

6 large firm tomatoes

¼ cup grated Parmesan cheese

¼ cup chopped fresh parsley

Fresh or dried basil

Salt and freshly ground pepper

¼ cup olive oil

Preheat the broiler.

Cut off the stem ends from each tomato and cut each tomato in half crosswise. Place each piece, cut side up, in a broiler pan. Top with 1 teaspoon of cheese and 1 teaspoon of parsley. Sprinkle with a little basil, salt, and pepper. Drizzle the tops with olive oil. Broil for 3 to 5 minutes or until bubbly.

Herbed Tomatoes

8 servings

4 large firm tomatoes

4 tablespoons unsalted butter

4 scallions, with some tops, minced

1 cup fine dry bread crumbs

¼ teaspoon dried basil or oregano

1 tablespoon chopped fresh parsley

Salt and freshly ground pepper

Preheat the oven to 350 degrees.

Cut the stem ends from the tomatoes and cut each tomato in half crosswise. Place cut side up in a shallow baking dish. In a small skillet melt the butter over medium-high heat. Add the scallions, bread crumbs, basil, and parsley. Season with salt and pepper and mix well. Spoon the mixture over the tomato halves, dividing it evenly. Bake for 15 minutes.

German Potato Pancakes

Kartoffelpuffer are internationally famous German creations made in a number of versions. They are often served with applesauce and as accompaniments to such meats as roast pork or sausages, but in the Alps are a favorite breakfast dish.

---

4 medium (about 1⅓ pounds) waxy potatoes

1 small white onion

1 large egg

2 tablespoons all-purpose flour

Salt and freshly ground pepper

Unsalted butter

Peel the potatoes and the onion and grate them into a large bowl. Drain off any liquid, pressing with a spoon to release all of it. Add the egg and flour and season with salt and pepper. Mix well. In a large skillet melt enough butter to grease the surface over medium-high heat. Drop spoonfuls of the potato mixture into the butter. Fry over medium-high heat for a few minutes to brown. With a spatula turn over pancakes and fry a few minutes to brown on the other side, adding more butter if needed. Serve at once.

114   **Cuisines of the Alps**

Italian Eggplant á la Parmigiana

This flavorful casserole is one of the best eggplant dishes, a favorite Italian vegetable. The handsome purple treasure, grown in round and elongated shapes, achieves added appeal when married with olive oil, tomatoes, and pungent herbs, as in this dish. In the Italian Alps it is served as a luncheon dish or accompaniment to roast meat, particularly lamb.

2 eggplants (about 1 pound each)

Salt

2 tablespoons olive oil, plus additional for frying

1 medium yellow onion, peeled and minced

1 (4-ounce) can tomato paste

1 teaspoon dried basil

1/2 teaspoon dried oregano

Freshly ground pepper

All-purpose flour

2 to 3 eggs, lightly beaten

3/4 pound mozzarella cheese, sliced

1/2 cup grated Parmesan cheese

Remove the stems from the eggplant and slice about 1/4 inch thick. Put in a colander and sprinkle with salt; drain for 30 minutes.

Meanwhile, in a large skillet heat 2 tablespoons olive oil over medium-high heat.

Add the onion and sauté for 4 minutes. Add the tomato paste, 1 1/2 cups water, basil, and oregano. Season with salt and pepper. Reduce heat to medium-low and cook, uncovered, stirring occasionally, 20 minutes.

Drain the eggplant and wipe dry with paper towels. Dredge each slice with flour and dip in the beaten egg. In a large skillet fry on both sides in hot oil over medium-high heat until golden. Drain on paper towels.

Preheat the oven to 350 degrees. Line a shallow baking dish with a little of the tomato sauce. Arrange a layer of eggplant slices over the sauce. Cover with a layer of mozzarella slices, one of sauce, and a sprinkling of Parmesan cheese. Repeat the layers until all the ingredients are used. Top with a generous sprinkling of Parmesan cheese. Bake about 30 minutes, until tender.

Sauerkraut

This is a very popular dish in Austria, Germany, Liechtenstein, and Slovenia. Fermented green cabbage or sauerkraut appears in a varied number of dishes. It may be simmered in white wine, beer, or bouillon; cooked with fruit, herbs, or spices; and appear as an accompaniment to or topped with meat or game. Visitors to the Alps are ever amazed at the interesting ways sauerkraut appears on their plates.

---

2 tablespoons bacon fat or vegetable oil

1 medium yellow onion, peeled and chopped

2 cups canned sauerkraut, drained

½ cup dry white wine

½ teaspoon caraway seeds

Salt and freshly ground pepper

1 medium waxy potato, peeled and grated

In a large saucepan heat the fat over medium-high heat. Add the onion and sauté for 4 minutes. Add the sauerkraut, wine, and caraway seeds. Season with salt and pepper. Reduce heat to medium-low and cook slowly, covered, 30 minutes. Add the grated potato and continue cooking, stirring occasionally for 30 minutes.

Kranjska Gora Sauerkraut Salad

6 to 8 servings

Known primarily for the best skiing in Slovenia and as an off-season sporting center, Kranjska Gora has hearty dishes featuring sauerkraut such as this salad. It is a good accompaniment to sausages, frankfurters, ham, or pork.

1 pound canned sauerkraut, drained and chopped

1 cup peeled, grated raw carrots

1 cup diced, cooked or canned beets, cold

¼ cup chopped celery

2 cups diced, peeled, cooked potatoes, cold

2 tablespoons minced gherkins

About ⅓ cup vegetable oil

2 tablespoons cider vinegar

2 teaspoons mustard

Salt and freshly ground pepper

3 tablespoons finely chopped fresh parsley

In a large bowl combine the sauerkraut, carrots, beets, celery, potatoes, and gherkins.

In a small bowl combine the oil, vinegar, and mustard. Season with salt and pepper. Add the vinaigrette to the sauerkraut mixture and mix well. Refrigerate, covered, 2 hours or longer to blend flavors. Serve sprinkled with parsley.

Mushroom Goulash

This is a good accompaniment for poultry or fish dishes.

---

3 tablespoons unsalted butter or vegetable oil

1 large yellow onion, peeled and chopped

1 tablespoon paprika

1 large green pepper, seeded and cut into strips

3 large tomatoes, peeled and chopped

1 pound mushrooms, thickly sliced

Salt and freshly ground pepper

In a large saucepan melt the butter or heat the oil over medium-high heat. Add the onion and sauté for 4 minutes. Add the paprika and cook 1 minute. Stir in the green pepper and tomatoes. Reduce the heat to medium-low and cook, uncovered, 10 minutes. Add the mushrooms and season with salt and pepper. Cook for 5 minutes.

Paprika Potatoes

In the Austrian Alps this is a basic dish to which tomatoes, green peppers, or sliced smoked sausages can be added.

3 tablespoons
vegetable oil

2 medium yellow
onions, peeled and
chopped

2 garlic cloves,
crushed

1 to 2 tablespoons
paprika

Salt and freshly
ground pepper

6 medium waxy
potatoes, peeled
and cubed

1 cup sour cream

In a medium saucepan heat the oil over medium-high heat. Add the onions and garlic and sauté for 4 minutes. Mix in the paprika and season with salt and pepper. Cook 2 minutes, then add the potatoes and enough water to barely cover. Reduce the heat to medium-low and cook, covered, for 20 minutes, until the potatoes are tender. Stir in the sour cream and heat on low heat until hot.

Slovenian Eggplant Stew

8 servings

In Slovenia a favorite way of preparing vegetables is to slowly cook one or more of them with seasonings into a flavorful stew. This dish has a rich, thick sauce. The recipe can also be prepared with green beans, okra, squash, or cauliflower and can be served hot or cold.

2 medium eggplants

1 cup olive oil

2 medium yellow onions, peeled and chopped

3 medium tomatoes, peeled and chopped

2 garlic cloves, crushed

¼ cup finely chopped fresh parsley

½ teaspoon dried marjoram

Salt and freshly ground pepper

Remove the stems from eggplants and cut into cubes. In a large saucepan heat the oil over medium-high heat. Add the onions and sauté for 5 minutes. Add the eggplant and sauté for 5 minutes. Stir in the tomatoes, garlic, parsley and marjoram. Season with salt and pepper. Reduce the heat to medium-low. Cook, covered, stirring several times, about 25 minutes, until the eggplant is tender.

Fennel with Parmesan

Fennel, an aromatic vegetable with an anise flavor, is highly regarded in Italy. Called finocchio, *the plant is valued for its seeds and leaves, used as seasonings, and for its bulb, which is used raw in salads or cooked in vegetable dishes. This is a favorite dish in the resort towns of the Italian Alps.*

---

4 bulbs fennel

Salt and freshly
  ground pepper

½ cup unsalted butter,
  melted

½ cup grated
  Parmesan cheese

Preheat the oven to 425 degrees. Butter a shallow baking dish.

Remove and discard the fernlike tops, tough outer stalks, and stems of the fennel. Wash the bulb and cut it crosswise into thin slices. In a large saucepan cook the fennel in boiling salted water to cover over medium-high heat until tender, about 5 minutes. Drain. Spoon the fennel into the prepared dish. Season with salt and pepper. Pour the melted butter over the fennel and sprinkle with cheese. Bake for about 10 minutes, until golden brown.

Tyrolean Creamed Spinach

4 to 6 servings

This is an interesting way of preparing spinach, a favorite Austrian vegetable.

---

2 (10-ounce) pack-
ages fresh spinach,
washed and
stemmed

Salt

2 tablespoons unsalted
butter

1 small onion, peeled
and minced

2 tablespoons
all-purpose flour

1/2 cup beef bouillon

1 tablespoon fresh
lemon juice

2 teaspoons chopped
fresh dill

Freshly ground pepper

1/2 cup sour cream, at
room temperature

In a large saucepan cook the spinach in a small amount of salted water over medium-high heat until tender. Drain the spinach and chop. Set aside.

In another saucepan melt butter over medium-high heat. Add onion and sauté for 4 minutes. Stir in the flour and cook 1 minute. Gradually add the bouillon and cook, stirring, until thickened. Reduce the heat to medium-low. Mix in the spinach, lemon juice, and dill. Season with salt and pepper. Stir in sour cream and heat for 2 to 3 minutes.

Swiss Rösti

Rösti or röesti, a Swiss potato dish, is made of cold cooked potatoes that are grated and then sautéed in butter so that they form a cake. In some versions grated cheese, onion, or ham is added to the potatoes.

6 medium (about 2 pounds) waxy potatoes, washed

Salt

1 small white onion, peeled and minced

About 4 tablespoons unsalted butter

In a medium saucepan cook the unpeeled potatoes in salted boiling water over medium-high heat until just tender, about 25 minutes. Drain, peel, and cool. Refrigerate the potatoes until chilled. Grate coarsely and mix with the onion. Season with salt.

In a medium skillet melt the butter over medium-high heat. Add the potato mixture. Flatten with a spatula into a thin cake and fry, until a golden crust forms on the bottom, about 7 minutes. Shake the pan occasionally so it does not stick. With a knife loosen around the edges. Put a plate over the top and invert onto the plate. Add more butter and then return the potato cake to the pan. Cook until golden brown on the other side. Slide the potato cake onto a warm plate.

Red Cabbage with Apples

4 to 6 servings

Purplish-red cabbage is used extensively in the Alpine cuisines, served especially with pork, game, or duck dishes.

1 red cabbage (about 2½ pounds), shredded

¾ cup boiling water

3 tart cooking apples, peeled, cored, and thinly sliced

3 tablespoons unsalted butter, melted

¼ cup cider or red wine vinegar

¼ cup brown sugar

Salt and freshly ground pepper

In a large saucepan combine the cabbage and boiling water over medium-high heat and cook, covered, 10 minutes. Add the apples and continue cooking for 10 minutes. In a small bowl combine the butter, vinegar, and sugar and add it to the cabbage mixture. Season with salt and pepper and cook 10 minutes longer.

Piedmont Truffles

A number of unusual dishes, including salads, are prepared with truffles, the mysterious fungi that grow underground, primarily in the Perigord region of France and the Piedmont district of Italy. Although they have been known for over two thousand years, they have never been successfully cultivated. Why and how they are grown has never been ascertained. To locate truffles, it's necessary to use trained pigs or dogs and root them from the ground..

Truffles are prized for their rarity, exceptional flavor, and remarkably penetrating aroma, which can overpower other foods. They vary in size and are usually black, dark brown, or "white" (actually cream-colored) but there are also pink and light-purple truffles.

In Alba, an animated little city with a long medieval pedestrian street, shop windows display the area's most prized product, the famous white truffle. Local restaurants serve pasta and risotto perfumed with shavings of the "little balls of fungi." There is also an annual truffle festival in October that includes a number of cultural events.

In Piedmont, an exceptional salad is made with white truffles and the highly prized soft, creamy fontina cheese, which stands up to the powerful truffle flavor, and a mustard cream dressing. The Viennese have a black-and-white salad made with truffles and potatoes.

Alpine Potato Salad

Alpine cooks have a great repertoire of potato salads, usually served as side dishes but sometimes as a simple entree on the supper table. Potato salad holds a place of honor at picnics and is greatly favored for summer outdoor meals. This recipe is flavored with dill and sour cream which is typical of the Alps.

---

4 medium waxy pota-
toes

Salt

1¼ cups sour cream,
at room temperature

2 tablespoons white
wine vinegar

½ teaspoon dried dill

Freshly ground pepper

½ cup diced green
pepper

½ cup diced celery

½ cup sliced scallions,
with some tops

3 hard-cooked eggs,
shelled and
chopped

¼ teaspoon paprika

1 large tomato,
peeled and cut into
wedges

In a medium saucepan cook the unpeeled potatoes in salted boiling water until tender, about 25 minutes. Drain, peel, and, while still warm, slice or cube the potatoes into a medium bowl. Add the sour cream, vinegar, and dill. Season with salt and pepper and mix well. Add the green pepper, celery, scallions, and eggs and mix well. Let the salad stand 1 hour or longer at room temperature to blend the flavors. Serve sprinkled with paprika and garnished with tomato wedges.

Gratin Dauphinois

One of the great dishes from Dauphine, *Gratin Dauphinois* is scalloped potatoes made with the local rich cream. It is prepared simply with raw potatoes, sliced as thinly as possible and put in a buttered shallow baking dish. After sprinkling with salt and pepper, and sometimes grated nutmeg, enough light cream is added to come just to the top layer. After dotting the surface with bits of butter, the potatoes are baked in a slow oven (250 degrees) about 1½ hours, or until most of the cream is absorbed and the potatoes are golden. Then the dish is returned to a 425 degree oven about 5 minutes to brown the top slightly.

Innsbruck Cucumber Salad

4 to 6 servings

Innsbruck, the capital of Austria's Tirol region in the Inn River valley, between the northern chain of the Alps and the Tuxer Mountains, is famous for its spectacular location, picturesque Old Town, and as a winter sports center. Gurkensalat is a popular Austrian salad that can be prepared in a number of inviting ways. Sometimes it is made with lemon juice instead of vinegar, without sugar, with garlic, or garnished with paprika. This is a traditional version.

---

3 medium cucumbers

Salt

¼ cup white wine vinegar

¼ cup vegetable oil

1 teaspoon sugar

Freshly ground white pepper

Sour cream (optional)

Chopped fresh chives or parsley

Peel the cucumbers and score with a fork. Cut into paper-thin slices. Put the cucumber in a bowl, sprinkle with salt, and set aside for 30 minutes. Drain well and place in a serving dish. Add the vinegar, oil, and sugar, and season with salt and pepper. Add the sour cream, if desired and mix well. Serve garnished with chives.

Italian Tomato-Bread Salad

4 servings

Italians are very fond of using dry bread in salads and soups. This favorite salad, panzanella, is made by moistening bread cubes with water and tossing them with tomatoes, onions, olive oil, and basil.

½ cup olive oil

3 tablespoons unsalted butter

1½ cups stale bread cubes

4 large tomatoes, peeled and sliced

1½ tablespoons wine vinegar

½ teaspoon dried basil

Salt and freshly ground pepper

2 tablespoons capers, drained

2 tablespoons chopped fresh parsley

Preheat the oven to 275 degrees.

In a medium skillet heat 3 tablespoons of the oil with the butter over medium-high heat. Add the bread cubes and sauté until golden brown. Put them in a shallow baking dish and bake for 25 minutes. Drain on absorbent paper.

In a salad bowl layer the bread cubes with the tomato slices. In a small bowl, combine the remaining 5 tablespoons oil, the vinegar, and basil, and season with salt and pepper. Spoon the vinaigrette over the tomato-bread mixture. Sprinkle with capers and parsley. Serve at once.

Austrian Red and White Coleslaw

4 to 6 servings

This salad made with red and green cabbage is a good accompaniment to schnitzels or other veal dishes.

2½ cups shredded green cabbage

1½ cups shredded red cabbage

2 tablespoons sugar

¼ cup French dressing (or mayonnaise)

¼ cup vegetable oil

2 to 3 tablespoons cider vinegar

¾ teaspoon celery seeds

Salt and freshly ground pepper

In a large bowl combine the green and red cabbage and the sugar. Refrigerate, covered, 1 hour. In a small bowl combine the French dressing, oil, vinegar, and celery seeds and season with salt and pepper. Add the dressing to the cabbage mixture and refrigerate for at least 2 hours to blend the flavors.

Onion-Watercress Salad

The Alpine countries have a fine repertoire of onion salads.
Some are simple dishes of sliced onions with one or more garnishes such as fresh herbs.
Others comprise a mixture of onions with colorful raw vegetables. This salad
featuring watercress is good served with meat or game.

1 bunch watercress

2 large red onions, peeled and thinly sliced

2 to 3 tablespoons olive oil

1 tablespoon white wine vinegar

½ teaspoon dried oregano or thyme

Salt and freshly ground pepper

4 flat anchovies, drained and chopped

8 black olives, pitted

Wash the watercress well to remove all dirt. Remove leaves from stems and discard any wilted leaves. Dry the leaves and refrigerate. When ready to serve, place watercress leaves on a plate and top with onion slices. Sprinkle the salad with oil, vinegar, and oregano and season with salt and pepper. Top with anchovies and garnish with olives.

Swiss Apple-Cheese Salad

The Swiss have created a fascinating number of salads combining cheese with raw vegetables and fruits that are served as a first course or side dish. This is a marvelous salad to serve at a family or children's supper.

---

4 red apples, unpeeled, cored and diced

2 tablespoons fresh lemon juice

1 cup diced celery

1 cup shredded Swiss cheese

About 1 cup mayonnaise

1 tablespoon mustard

Salt and freshly ground pepper

Lettuce leaves, washed and dried

½ cup chopped walnuts

Put the apples in a serving dish and sprinkle with lemon juice. Add the celery and cheese. In a small bowl, combine the mayonnaise and mustard and season with salt and pepper. Add the dressing to the apple mixture. Refrigerate for 1 hour to blend flavors. Serve on lettuce leaves, sprinkled with nuts.

Cheese Salad

This is another excellent Swiss salad made with cheese.

¾ pound Swiss
  cheese, cut into
  ½-inch cubes

½ cup chopped
  scallions, with
  some tops

1 tablespoon prepared
  horseradish

1 tablespoon white
  vinegar

2 tablespoons
  vegetable oil

2 teaspoons mustard

2 tablespoons
  mayonnaise

Salt and freshly
  ground pepper

Lettuce leaves

tomato slices,
  to garnish

gherkin slices,
  to garnish

In a bowl combine the cheese and scallions. In another small bowl, mix together the horseradish, vinegar, oil, mustard, and mayonnaise, and season with salt and pepper. Mix the dressing with the cheese mixture. Refrigerate the salad for 2 hours to blend the flavors. To serve, place the salad on lettuce leaves and garnish with the tomato and gherkin slices.

Hop Sprouts

Hop sprouts, called *jets de houblon* in French and *Hopfenspresson* in German, are the edible flowers of a perennial herb important to the brewing of ale and beer. The young shoots are cut in spring from tall climbing vines, and are considered great delicacies in France and Germany. They are boiled and served with butter and cream, with herbed sauces, or cold as a salad. Hops can be prepared in the same way as asparagus and are especially good with lemon-flavored mayonnaise, hollandaise, or vinaigrette. In one Bavarian salad, the hops are combined with chopped cooked ham, hard-cooked eggs, and tomatoes, bound with mayonnaise, and served on watercress. In markets such as those in Munich and some areas of the United States, the sprouts are available for a few weeks in spring.

To cook, boil the sprouts in a little salted water with a few drops of lemon juice until tender. Drain and cool. Serve as suggested above.

Italian Cardoon Salad

The cardoon, a thistle-like plant related to the artichoke but similar in appearance to a large bunch of celery, is whitish-green with a delicate and slightly bitter taste. It has a thick skin and outer stalks that must be removed before cooking, as only the inner stalks are edible. Smaller plants are preferable for salads. A cardoon must be blanched or pre-cooked, and, once cut, it should be rubbed with lemon juice or put in acidulated water to prevent discoloring.

---

2 bunches cardoons

3 to 4 tablespoons fresh lemon juice or vinegar

Salt

½ pound mushrooms, sliced

⅓ cup olive oil

½ teaspoon dried oregano

Salt and freshly ground pepper

2 medium tomatoes, peeled and cut into wedges

2 hard-cooked eggs, shelled and quartered

Remove tough outer and wilted stalks of cardoons. Remove all leaves and strings from inner stalks and cut into 3-inch pieces. Trim the hearts and cut into pieces. To keep the cardoon from darkening, immediately drop the cut pieces into cold water with a little lemon juice or vinegar. In a medium saucepan cook the cardoons in boiling salted water, covered, over medium-high heat, about 10 minutes, until just tender. Drain and cool. Combine the cardoons with the mushrooms in a serving dish. Sprinkle with oil, lemon juice, oregano, salt, and pepper. Serve garnished with tomatoes and eggs.

Liechtenstein Corn-Bean Salad

4 to 6 servings

This is an appealing salad from the tiny Alpine principality of Liechtenstein. It is a good dish to serve as an accompaniment to any kind of meat or poultry.

1 cup fresh cooked or drained canned corn

2 cups cooked kidney beans, drained

1 cup peeled, diced cucumber

1 medium onion, peeled and diced

2 medium tomatoes, peeled and chopped

3 tablespoons olive oil

1 tablespoon cider vinegar

2 tablespoons minced fresh parsley

Salt and freshly ground pepper

Crisp lettuce leaves

In a medium bowl combine the corn, beans, cucumber, onion, and tomatoes. Add the oil, vinegar, and parsley, and season with salt and pepper. Refrigerate the salad 2 to 3 hours to blend flavors. To serve, place the lettuce leaves in a bowl. Top with the salad mixture.

Pasta, Rice, and Other Grains

Edible seeds of the grass family, more commonly known as cereals or grains, have played a fascinating variety of gastronomic roles in man's diet. In Alpine countries, oats, wheat, barley, and rye and, to a lesser extent, rice and corn, have provided necessary daily sustenance for the populace. Fortunately, inventive cooks utilize these foods to create a wide selection of such culinary treasures as pasta, risotto, and polenta, among others.

The history of civilization is intertwined with the quest for rich grain-bearing lands and the crops they yielded. Ancient Romans introduced the cultivation of grains throughout Europe where these foods also became basic and essential fare. During and long after the Middle Ages, pottages, gruels, and soups, thickened and enriched with grains, were often consumed three times daily.

One of the earliest of the great grain dishes was made with a particular hard durum wheat called semolina, which when mixed with water, rolled and dried, became what we call pasta. As early as 500 B.C. the Italians were making spaghetti, macaroni, noodles, and possibly other kinds of pasta. The Historical Museum of Spaghetti in Pontedassio, Liguria, contains displays documents proving the ancient origin of this popular food. Over the years Italians created many additional kinds of pasta, perhaps 100 different varieties, and by the 1500s their popularity had spread to other European countries.

In the northern provinces of Italy, Lombardy, Piedmont, and Veneto, rice is a most important ingredient in a number of excellent dishes, especially risotto. Although rice dishes appear on the menus of Alpine restaurants and are eaten in many homes, this grain never became staple fare throughout the area. Their varied preparations, however, are well worth savoring.

Such staple creations as dumplings, fritters, and pancakes, are also included here, as they were developed into inviting creations by cooks who sought to vary the use of finely ground grains.

This characteristic and pleasing recipe collection reflects the many ways that the fruits of the field have been upgraded from basic fare to a position of esteem in the Alpine cuisine.

Pasta

In the culinary repertoire pasta might well be deemed the perfect player. Healthful, nourishing, inexpensive, and easy to prepare, it is the hostess's boon and the guests' delight. Pasta may be the prologue to an entrancing meal, lend support to other dishes with remarkable versatility, or star as the main attraction. Whether it is in the form of spaghetti, macaroni, shells, rigatoni, letters, vermicelli, lasagna, or egg noodles, pasta lends sustenance and charm to everyday or company meals, so it's no small wonder that it is one of the world's most popular foods, including in the Alpine countries. For all its accommodating versatility, however, pasta is proud and demands proper preparation. Overcooked and over seasoned, served without thought or attention, it becomes a soggy, sticky mess. Proper cooking of the pasta is most important. Thus, directions for its preparation should be followed carefully.

Egg Pasta

Basic fresh egg-pasta, called pasta fresca all'uovo *in Italy, is used to make a number of types of noodles and other dishes by cutting the sheet of dough into contrasting shapes. The simplest of the Italian repertoire is tagliatelle, a name derived from* tagliare, *meaning "to cut." Thus there are several noodles with names beginning with* taglia, *all of the same "family," which differ only in their width. Americans are more familiar with another name for the same noodle, fettuccine, which is used in Rome and southern Italy.*

---

3 cups semolina or all-purpose flour

3 eggs, at room temperature

¾ teaspoon salt

2 teaspoons olive or vegetable oil

¼ cup lukewarm water, approximately

Sift the flour into a large bowl or onto a wooden or marble surface to form a mound. Make a well or depression in the center, and carefully break the eggs into it. Add the salt and oil. Working with tips of the fingers, mix the flour with the other ingredients to combine well. Add the water a little at a time, as needed, to make a stiff paste that forms a compact ball. Knead the dough on a floured surface until it is smooth and elastic, 5 to 10 minutes. Set the dough aside, covered, to rest for 15 to 30 minutes. Divide the dough in half and roll out each portion on a lightly floured board, turning often and dusting with flour, if needed, until very thin, between ⅛ and 1/16 inch thick. Cut the pasta according to the following directions.

Tagliatelle: Roll each sheet of dough into a jelly-roll shape, and with a sharp knife slice crosswise into strips ranging ⅛ to ½ inch wide. Unroll each strip and place on a clean towel to dry for 1 hour. (Unroll quickly before they stick together.) Cook several pieces of pasta at a time in a pot of boiling salted water until just tender. Drain. Serve at once.

Fettuccine: Prepare and cook in the same fashion as tagliatelle, but cut the strips ¼ to ½ inch wide.

Lasagna: Cut the dough into 3-inch strips about 6 inches long. Dry, covered, for 1 hour. Cook in boiling salted water with a little oil until just tender. Drain. Use in a baked dish.

Cannelloni: Cut the dough into 4½ x 5-inch rectangles. Dry, covered, for 1 hour. Drop a few at a time into boiling salted water, and cook until just tender. Remove carefully and drain. Cool before filling and rolling.

Manicotti: Cut the dough into 3-inch squares. Dry, covered, for 1 hour. Drop a few at a time into boiling salted water, and cook until just tender. Remove carefully and drain. Cool before filling and rolling.

Pasta with Salsa Pomodoro

4 to 6 servings

In Italy the tomato became known as pomodoro, *meaning "golden apple," probably because those first introduced to Europe from the New World were small and yellow. Today, bright red tomatoes are grown in great quantity in Italy and are commonly used in the cookery, particularly with pasta as in this dish, commonly prepared in the Alps.*

3 tablespoons olive oil

1 cup chopped yellow onions

2 small garlic coves, crushed or minced

2 tablespoons chopped bacon

1 medium carrot, peeled and minced

1 medium stalk celery, cleaned and minced

3½ cups peeled and chopped fresh tomatoes

1 teaspoon dried basil

Salt and freshly ground pepper

⅓ cup chopped fresh parsley

1 pound pasta (spaghetti, macaroni or noodles), cooked and drained

⅓ cup unsalted butter

½ cup grated Romano or Parmesan cheese

In a large saucepan combine the oil, onions, garlic, bacon, carrot, and celery over medium-low heat. Cook, stirring often, for 5 minutes. Add the tomatoes and basil. Season with salt and pepper. Mix well; cook slowly, uncovered, for 1 hour, or until very thick. Stir in the parsley. In a large serving dish combine the pasta with the butter and cheese. Pour hot tomato sauce over it. Serve at once.

Italian Vegetable Spaghetti

4 servings

A typical Italian and Alpine way of cooking pasta is with vegetables such as eggplant, green peas, zucchini, or broccoli.

---

3 tablespoons olive oil

2 tablespoons unsalted butter

1 or 2 garlic cloves, crushed or minced

2 medium tomatoes, peeled and chopped

3 cups cubed eggplant or zucchini, cut up broccoli, or green peas

½ cup chicken broth

½ teaspoon dried basil

Salt and freshly ground pepper

1 pound spaghetti, cooked and drained

½ cup grated Parmesan cheese

In a large saucepan heat the oil and butter over medium-high heat. Add garlic and tomatoes. Cook 1 or 2 minutes. Add the vegetables, broth, and basil. Season with salt and pepper. Reduce heat to medium-low. Cook slowly, covered, until the vegetables are tender, about 15 minutes. In a large bowl toss the vegetable mixture with the hot spaghetti. Sprinkle with the cheese.

Swiss Macaroni and Cheese

*Macaroni and cheese is a favorite combination in all Alpine countries,
made in interesting variations. This version is superb as the macaroni is served with
the traditional Swiss garnish of onions fried in butter and mixed with cheese.*

---

8 ounces elbow
  macaroni

Salt

6 tablespoons unsalted
  butter

2½ cups thinly sliced
  yellow onions

1½ cups stale bread
  cubes

½ cup grated Swiss
  cheese

In a large saucepan cook the macaroni in salted boiling water until just tender; drain. Meanwhile, in a medium skillet melt 3 tablespoons of the butter over medium-high heat. Add the onions; sauté until deep golden and limp. Remove with a slotted spoon to a plate. Add the remaining 3 tablespoons butter and the bread cubes to the skillet. Sauté until golden. Combine the drained, cooked macaroni with the onions and bread cubes in the skillet. Add cheese; toss with two forks to mix well. Serve at once.

Alpine Fettuccine with Cheese

6 servings

One of the best and most famous egg noodle dishes is called fettuccine. Homemade fettuccine are preferable, but those sold fresh in Italian or specialty food stores or packaged dry medium egg noodles can be used.

---

1 pound fettuccine or medium egg noodles

Salt

½ cup (1 stick) unsalted butter, softened

1 cup heavy cream, warm

Freshly ground white pepper

2 cups grated Parmesan cheese, preferably freshly grated

In a large saucepan cook the fettuccine or noodles in salted boiling water until just tender, allowing about 5 minutes for the fettuccine and 8 for the noodles. Drain. Spoon at once into a large skillet over medium-low heat. Add butter; stir gently with the noodles until it melts. Add cream and pepper. Toss with two large forks. Add 1 cup of the cheese. Continue tossing all the ingredients until well mixed and hot. Serve remaining 1 cup cheese separately to be sprinkled over the noodles at the table.

German Baked Noodles and Applesauce

The Germans enjoy sweet noodle dishes like this one as accompaniments to meats and poultry or for supper with sliced cold sausages.

---

1 package (8 ounces) wide egg noodles

Salt

2 eggs, lightly beaten

½ cup light cream or milk

¼ cup (½ stick) unsalted butter, plus 2 tablespoons

1 cup seedless raisins

2 jars (1 pound each) applesauce

⅔ cup sugar

1 teaspoon grated lemon rind

1 teaspoon ground cinnamon

Fine dry bread crumbs

Preheat the oven to 375 degrees. Butter a 1½-quart baking dish

Cook noodles in salted boiling water according to package directions until tender. Drain. Turn at once into a large bowl. Add eggs, cream, butter, and raisins. Mix well. In another bowl combine the applesauce, sugar, lemon rind, and cinnamon. Arrange noodle and applesauce mixtures in layers in prepared baking dish. Sprinkle the top with bread crumbs; dot with butter. Bake 30 to 40 minutes, until cooked.

Risotto á la Milanese

8 servings

In Milan, northern Italy's thriving and most important city, one of the best known rice dishes is prepared with the fine grains grown in the nearby Po Valley of Lombardy. It is rich, creamy, and flavored with saffron. Italians enjoy the specialty as an accompaniment to meat, poultry, game, and seafood.

---

8 tablespoons (1 stick) unsalted butter

1 cup finely chopped yellow onions

2 cups short or medium grain rice

1 cup dry white wine

2 cups hot well-seasoned chicken broth

Salt and freshly ground pepper

$\frac{1}{8}$ teaspoon saffron, powdered or crumbled

$\frac{1}{4}$ cup freshly grated Parmesan cheese

In a large skillet melt 6 tablespoons of the butter over medium-high heat. Add the onion; sauté 4 minutes. Stir in the rice; sauté about 5 minutes, until the rice is coated with butter. Turn the heat to high; pour in wine. Cook, stirring often, over high heat until most of the wine has evaporated. Add 1 cup of the hot broth. Season with salt and pepper. Reduce the heat a little. Continue cooking, uncovered, stirring frequently, until most of the liquid has been absorbed. While cooking, add remaining broth, $\frac{1}{2}$ cup at a time, stirring to be sure the mixture does not stick to the pan. The whole cooking process will take about 30 minutes, possibly a bit longer. The resulting risotto should be creamy, with the tender grains.

Meanwhile, steep the saffron in a little hot water for about a minute. When the rice is cooked, mix in remaining 2 tablespoons butter, the Parmesan cheese, and saffron. Serve at once.

Lombardy Risotto with Zucchini

6 servings

The Lombardy region in northern Italy stretches south from the fringes of the Alps to the River Po. It is known for its breathtaking beauty, lakes, and rice dishes such as this zucchini risotto.

---

3 small zucchini
(about 1 pound)

5 tablespoons unsalted
butter

½ cup minced yellow
onions

1 or 2 garlic cloves,
crushed

1 cup short or
medium-grain rice

4 cups chicken broth,
hot

1 cup finely chopped
fresh parsley

Salt and freshly
ground pepper

¼ cup grated
Parmesan cheese

Remove the stems from the zucchini; wipe dry; thinly slice. In a large skillet melt 2 tablespoons of the butter over medium-high heat. Add the zucchini slices; sauté 2 or 3 minutes, until golden. With a slotted spoon remove and set aside. Add 2 more tablespoons butter to the skillet. Add onions and garlic; sauté 5 minutes. Add rice; sauté until grains become golden. Pour in 2 cups of the broth. Cook, uncovered, stirring occasionally, 10 minutes. Add 1 more cup of broth, the zucchini, and parsley. Season with salt and pepper. Continue cooking until all the liquid is absorbed. Add remaining 1 cup broth. Continue cooking a little longer, until the rice is just tender. Stir in the remaining 1 tablespoon butter and the cheese. Serve while still moist and creamy.

Austrian Poppy Seed Noodles

4 servings

Austrians enjoy a sweet noodle dish such as this one as an accompaniment to cold meats or poultry.

---

8 ounces fine egg noodles

¼ cup (½ stick) unsalted butter

3 tablespoons ground poppy seeds

3 tablespoons sugar

½ teaspoon grated lemon rind

In a large saucepan cook noodles in salted boiling water over medium-high heat until tender. Drain; turn into a warm bowl. Stir in butter; mix with hot noodles until butter melts. Meanwhile, in a small dish combine poppy seeds, sugar, and grated lemon. Sprinkle over the noodles. Serve at once.

Note: Finely chopped nuts such as walnuts or hazelnuts may be substituted for the poppy seeds, if desired.

Bread Dumplings

6 servings

The Germans as well as the Austrians and Slovenes are true devotees of dumplings which they make in great variety and consume daily in large quantity. Knödel are made with flour, potatoes, or bread cubes, and can include such ingredients as fruit or liver. They are eaten as accompaniments to meats and for dessert.

3 cups stale white (½-inch) bread cubes

½ cup milk

3 thin slices bacon, finely chopped

1 small onion, peeled and minced

2 eggs, lightly beaten

2 tablespoons chopped fresh parsley

About 1¾ cups sifted all-purpose flour

Place bread cubes in a large bowl. Cover with milk. In a medium skillet fry the bacon until crisp over medium-high heat. Remove bacon; pour off all except 1 tablespoon of fat. Add onion; sauté 3 minutes. Add cooked bacon, onion, eggs, and parsley to bread cubes. Mix well. Stir in enough flour to make a stiff dough; beat well. With floured hands, shape dough into six balls. Drop into a large kettle of boiling salted water. Boil, uncovered, until dumplings rise to the top. Cover; cook 10 to 15 minutes, or until done. Test by tearing one apart with two forks. Remove with a slotted spoon; drain.

Miniature Dumplings

Tiny noodles called späetzle, served in soups or as accompaniments to meats, poultry, game, or stews, are specialties of the inviting Swabian region of Germany and are also popular in Bavaria. The name means "tiny sparrows" and it is considered both a dumpling and a noodle. Made in infinite variety, the little balls of dough may include minced cooked ham, spinach, or cheese, and can be served with gravy, or tossed with mushrooms. This is a basic recipe.

2½ cups sifted
  all-purpose flour
½ teaspoon salt
2 eggs, lightly beaten
Water
Butter, melted
  (optional)

Sift flour and salt into a large bowl. Make a well in the center; add eggs and ½ cup water. Stir, adding more water as necessary, to make a stiff dough. Beat with a wooden spoon until soft and light. Let the dough stand for 30 minutes. Dampen a wooden board and turn the dough out onto it. Roll out to a thickness of about ⅛ inch. With a sharp wet knife cut small strips or slivers of the dough. Drop several pieces at a time into boiling salted water in a medium saucepan over medium-high heat. Cook until the noodles rise to the surface, 3 to 5 minutes. With a slotted spoon remove the noodles from the water; drain. Proceed with remaining dough. Serve at once or sauté in melted butter before serving, if desired.

Italian Spinach Dumplings

4 to 6 servings

Although Italians are not generally regarded as dumpling devotees, they do have a very popular kind called gnocchi. Most are preparations of potatoes and flour, but some include cheese, or like this one, spinach and cheese. Like pasta, they may be served as a first course, or as an accompaniment to meats.

---

1 package (10 ounces) fresh spinach or 1 package (10 ounces) frozen spinach

½ cup ricotta or cottage cheese

1 egg, lightly beaten

½ cup freshly grated Parmesan cheese

¼ to ⅓ cup all-purpose flour

Freshly grated nutmeg

Salt and freshly ground pepper

¼ cup unsalted butter, melted

If fresh spinach is used, clean, wash, and chop. If using frozen, thaw and chop. In a large saucepan cook the spinach with only the water clinging to the fresh leaves (or add a small amount of water to the frozen) over medium-low heat for a few minutes, until wilted. Drain off all the liquid, pressing firmly with a spoon. In a large bowl combine the spinach, ricotta cheese, egg, ¼ cup of the Parmesan cheese, ¼ cup of the flour, and the nutmeg. Season with salt and pepper. Add a little more flour if necessary to make a thick dough. Chill in the refrigerator for 1 hour.

With floured hands, form into 1¼-inch balls. Roll each one in flour. Chill again for 30 minutes.

Preheat the oven to 450 degrees and grease an 8-inch baking dish. Heat a saucepan of salted water to simmering over medium-low heat. Gently drop dough balls into the water, a few at a time. Remove with a slotted spoon to the prepared dish. When all are cooked, pour the melted butter and remaining ¼ cup of Parmesan over the gnocchi. Put in oven for 5 minutes.

Piedmont Polenta

After its introduction from America, corn became popular in the northern Italian region of Piedmont. There the staple dish is polenta, an Italian word for cornmeal and dishes made with it. Polenta is usually yellow, but sometimes white, coarsely or finely ground, and, when cooked, may be eaten soft and hot or cooled and firm.

---

1 teaspoon salt

1½ cups finely ground polenta or yellow cornmeal

In a large saucepan combine 6 cups water and the salt; bring to a boil over medium-high heat. Slowly pour the polenta into the boiling water, stirring continuously to prevent lumping, and being sure the water continues to boil. When the mixture is smooth, lower the heat and cook, uncovered, stirring frequently, about 30 minutes or until it is thick. A good test is to see if a wooden stirring spoon will stand without falling in center of the mush. Serve at once with butter and grated Parmesan cheese. Or, spoon into a greased 8-inch round or rectangular baking dish; chill for 1 hour or until very firm. Slice or cut into pieces. Fry, bake, or grill and serve with butter and cheese or a warm tomato or meat sauce.

Ticino Cornmeal-Cheese Casserole

In the Swiss canton of Ticino, a vacation paradise south of the Alps, where tourists flock to the cities of Lugano, Locarno, and Ascona, there are many noteworthy culinary specialties that originated in Italy. Polenta is one of these and the Swiss have created some different ways of serving it such as this dish. It is a good accompaniment to meats, particularly pork or sausages.

1 teaspoon salt

1½ cups polenta or
   yellow cornmeal

Unsalted butter, melted

Gruyère cheese, grated

Tomato slices

Preheat the oven to 375 degrees and grease an 8-inch baking dish.

In a large saucepan combine 6 cups water and the salt. Bring to a boil over medium-high heat. Slowly pour polenta into the boiling water, stirring as adding to prevent any lumping. The water should continue to boil. When mixture is smooth, lower the heat and cook, uncovered and stirring often, about 30 minutes, or until the mixture is thickened and set. Let cool. Cut into slices. Put in the prepared dish in layers, each sprinkled with melted butter, grated cheese, and tomato slices. Bake for 25 minutes.

Desserts

While dining in Alpine countries it is always difficult to choose among the inviting and delectable pastries, puddings, ice creams, cheese, and fruit specialties for dessert. Fortunately, one is not limited to enjoying them all at the end of a meal. For it is it is customary to partake of toothsome sweets, handsomely displayed in bakeries, pastry shops, and confectioners' stores, throughout the day and evening or as snacks.

The word dessert derives from the French verb, *desservir*, meaning "to clear the table." At one time in Europe it was customary to offer an elaborate presentation of sweets after everything had been removed from the dining table. Now the selection is confined to one or a few dishes, but each will be a superb creation prepared with only the very best ingredients. Alpine cooks take great pride in making and serving their illustrious national specialties.

The first Alpine desserts were probably puddings made by combining grains, fruits, and nuts, sweetened with wine and honey. Gradually, over the years, cooks developed more refinements in the art of making such desserts as pastries, custards, cheesecakes, and particularly those featuring fruit. The extensive orchards yielded an increasing variety of delectable fruit, which was fashioned into compotes, tarts, pies, cakes, dumplings, fried batters, and confections that are still relished today. Candied fruits are also widely enjoyed. The peels of such favorites as oranges and lemons are extensively utilized in the cookery.

Throughout the Alpine regions the choice of a typical dessert varies considerably. In Italy light desserts such as fruit, cheese, or custards are preferred. Sweets are eaten, however, with morning coffee or as snacks at other times. The Austrians, Germans, and Slovenes are particularly fond of sweet dumplings, pancakes, cakes, and such pastries as strudel and torte.

Of all the great Alpine desserts particular mention should be made of the ices and ice creams that appear as glorious creations in every cuisine. Since the days of the Romans, iced fruit-flavored waters have been considered luxurious fare. To keep them cool, the Romans devised a system of preserving ice during the hot summer months. From the Arabs, the Italians learned the secrets of preparing *sharbats* (sherbets) and sorbets, and introduced them to other Europeans. Once the consistency of these treasures had been strengthened with the addition of eggs and cream, the repertoire of frozen desserts knew no bounds.

German Apple Pancakes

Sweetened apple-filled pancakes called Apfelpfannkuchen *are a favorite German dessert, always on the restaurant menus in Mittenwald, one of the most spectacular locations in the Bavarian Alps. Once an important center for Alpine commerce, it is world famous for violin making and its Violin Making Museum.*

---

6 tablespoons unsalted butter

4 tart apples, peeled and thinly sliced

2 teaspoons grated lemon peel

½ to ¾ cup granulated sugar

1 teaspoon ground cinnamon

1 cup sifted all-purpose flour

¼ teaspoon salt

1 cup milk

2 eggs, lightly beaten

Confectioners' sugar

Preheat the oven to 250 degrees.

In a medium skillet melt 4 tablespoons of the butter over medium-low heat. Add the apple slices. Cook, stirring, until apples are soft. Don't overcook. Add lemon peel, granulated sugar to taste, and cinnamon. Mix well. Leave in the skillet over very low heat.

Meanwhile, in a medium bowl combine the flour, salt, milk, and eggs. Whisk until smooth. Melt the remaining 2 tablespoons butter; add to flour mixture. Mix well.

In a lightly greased 7- or 8-inch skillet over medium-high heat, add 3 tablespoons batter. Tilt pan at once to spread the batter evenly. Cook until underside of pancake is golden. With a spatula turn over; cook on the other side. Turn out onto a warm plate. Keep warm in oven. Continue cooking remaining pancakes. Spread half of each one with a thin layer of the warm apple mixture. Fold over. Sprinkle with confectioners' sugar. Serve at once.

Italian Zabaglione

This popular wine-flavored custard is sometimes also called zabaione. It is made in several variations and is sometimes used as a sauce. The French have an adaptation of it, which they call saboyan.

---

4 egg yolks
¼ cup granulated sugar
¾ cup Marsala wine

In the top of a double boiler over simmering water, combine the egg yolks and sugar. Beat with a wire whisk or rotary beater until foamy. Gradually add the Marsala. Continue beating until mixture thickens. Spoon at once into stemmed glasses and serve.

Slovenian Baked Pancakes

Makes about 14

This is one of the many pancake desserts that are beloved fare in Slovenia.

---

2 eggs, lightly beaten

1½ cups milk

¼ teaspoon salt

1 tablespoon
granulated sugar

2 teaspoons grated
lemon peel

1½ cups all-purpose
flour

Unsalted butter

Raspberry or
strawberry jam
or jelly

Slivered almonds

Confectioners' sugar

1 cup light cream

Preheat the oven to 250 degrees. Grease an 11¾ x 7½ baking dish.

In a large bowl combine eggs, milk, salt, granulated sugar, and lemon peel. Stir in flour; mix well. In a 7- or 8-inch skillet melt 2 to 3 tablespoons butter over medium-high heat. Add 3 tablespoons batter; quickly tilt pan to spread evenly. Cook until underside is golden. Turn over; cook on other side. Turn out onto a warm plate. Keep warm in oven. Continue cooking remaining pancakes. Spread each one with jam; sprinkle with almonds and confectioners' sugar. Roll up; place, folded sides underneath, side by side, in the prepared dish. Cover with cream. Turn up oven heat to 350 degrees. Cover th pan with foil and bake for 20 minutes.

Baked Apricots

4 servings

It's a great pleasure to dine in the Italian village of Courmayeur, a summer and winter resort on the southeastern side of Mont Blanc and a spa destination since the 1600s. It is known today for its attractive narrow cobbled streets, cafés, lively festivals, and restaurants that serve one of region's great treasures, flavorful fresh fruit, especially peaches and apricots, which are made into compotes, tarts, ice cream, or this appealing dessert.

---

12 ripe apricots

Lemon juice

¾ cup granulated
  sugar

1 teaspoon vanilla

Whipped cream

Preheat the oven to 350 degrees.

Peel the apricots. Cut into halves along their natural lines. Remove pits. Sprinkle with a little lemon juice. In a small saucepan combine the sugar, 1 cup water, and vanilla over medium-high heat. Bring to a boil. Reduce heat to medium-low. Simmer 5 minutes. Arrange apricots in a shallow baking dish. Pour syrup over them. Bake for 45 to 55 minutes, until fork-tender. Cool. Then chill in refrigerator. Serve with whipped cream.

Cuisines of the Alps

Jam-Filled Pancakes

This is another of the typical Alpine dessert pancakes.

2 eggs, separated

½ cup milk

1 tablespoon granulated sugar

¼ teaspoon salt

2 tablespoons brandy or rum

1 cup all-purpose flour

Unsalted butter for frying

Fruit jam

Confectioners' sugar

Preheat the oven to 250 degrees.

In a large bowl combine the egg yolks, milk, ½ cup water, granulated sugar, salt, and brandy. Stir in flour; mix well. In another bowl beat the egg whites until stiff; fold into flour mixture.

In a 7- or 8-inch skillet melt a little butter over medium-high heat. Add 3 tablespoons batter. Tilt pan at once to spread the batter evenly. Reduce heat to medium-low. Cook until underside is golden. With a spatula flip the pancake and cook on other side. Turn out onto a warm plate. Keep warm in the oven. Continue cooking the remaining pancakes. Spread each pancake with a thin layer of jam; fold into quarters. Serve at once sprinkled with confectioners' sugar.

Wine Cream

A favorite German dessert is a chilled Weincreme. *The same mixture may be served warm as a sauce over plain cake.*

---

2 cups dry white wine

1/2 cup granulated sugar

4 eggs, lightly beaten

1 teaspoon grated lemon peel

1 teaspoon grated orange peel

Whipped cream (optional)

In the top of a double boiler over medium-high heat combine the wine, sugar, eggs, and lemon and orange peels. Cook, beating with a whisk or fork, until frothy and thickened. Pour into serving dishes. Chill. Serve topped with whipped cream, if desired.

Slovenian Rice Pudding

4 to 6 servings

Cold milk puddings garnished with finely chopped nuts or ground cinnamon are favorite desserts and snacks in Slovenia.

⅓ cup long-grain rice
3 tablespoons cornstarch
4 cups milk
⅓ cup granulated sugar
1 cinnamon stick
Finely chopped nuts or ground cinnamon

In a medium saucepan combine the rice and 1 cup water over medium-high heat. Cook, covered, about 20 minutes, until liquid is absorbed and grains are tender. In a small dish combine the cornstarch with ½ cup of the milk. In a large saucepan over medium-low heat combine the cornstarch mixture with remaining 3½ cups milk, the cooked rice, sugar, and cinnamon stick. Cook, stirring frequently, until pudding is thickened. Remove and discard cinnamon stick. Spoon into small bowls. Chill. Serve garnished with nuts or cinnamon.

Chocolate Pots de Creme

This elegant French rich chocolate custard is served in little covered pots called petits pots. *If not available, other small containers may be used.*

2 cups light cream

6 egg yolks

2 tablespoons granulated sugar

Pinch of salt

6 ounces semisweet chocolate, grated

1 teaspoon vanilla

Whipped cream (optional)

In a medium saucepan heat the cream over medium-high heat until bubbles appear around the edge. Meanwhile, in a large bowl combine the egg yolks, sugar, and salt but do not beat. Pour $\frac{1}{3}$ of the hot cream mixture into the egg mixture. Stir; pour into the cream mixture in the saucepan. Cook, stirring constantly, over medium-low heat until mixture thickens and the spoon is coated. Stir in the grated chocolate. Remove from the heat. Keep stirring until chocolate melts. Add vanilla. Pour into 8 small ($\frac{1}{3}$ cup) pots de creme, demitasse cups, or small bowls. Chill. Serve garnished with a dab of whipped cream, if desired.

Italian Citrus Granita

In Italy there are two kinds of ice cream. Gelati *is similar to the American ice cream and* granita *is a kind of sherbet that has fine ice crystals. This is particularly refreshing.*

---

1 cup granulated
  sugar

6 tablespoons fresh
  lemon juice

6 tablespoons fresh
  orange juice

1 teaspoon grated
  lemon peel

In a medium saucepan combine 2 cups water and sugar over medium-high heat. Bring to a boil. Cook over fairly high heat for 5 minutes. Remove from heat; cool. Add lemon and orange juice and grated lemon peel. Pour into a refrigerator tray. Freeze until firm and granular, about 4 to 6 hours.

Salzburger Nockerln

Salzburg, the birth city of Mozart and home to a famous annual music festival, lies on the very edge of the Alps. The city is steeped in history and alive with culture. Among the many attractions are charming winding streets, grand squares, and fashionable cafés with tempting Austrian desserts, including the city's most famous creation, Salzburger Nockerln. It was created over 275 years ago by a chef in the Hohensalzburg Palace. It is said that there are as many recipes for the dessert as there are people in the city.

½ cup milk

1 to 2 tablespoons granulated sugar

½ teaspoon vanilla

4 eggs, separated

3 tablespoons confectioners' sugar, plus additional for dusting

1 teaspoon all-purpose flour

Preheat the oven to 375 degrees.

Butter a square or oval 8- or 9-inch baking dish. Combine the milk, granulated sugar, and vanilla in the pan; stir well. Put in oven for 5 minutes.

Meanwhile, beat egg whites in a large bowl until soft peaks form. Add the confectioners' sugar, 1 spoonful at a time, beating after each addition, until the mixture is thick and glossy. In a small dish combine the egg yolks and flour. Add to egg white mixture. Remove heated milk mixture from the oven. With a spatula, drop three large mounds of egg mixture into the milk, making them wide and high. Return to oven for 8 to 10 minutes, or until outside is golden and puffed and inside is soft and creamy. Dust with confectioners' sugar. Serve at once.

Emperor's Pancake

This excellent and traditional Austrian dessert called Kaiserschmarrn, *often translated as the Kaiser's or emperor's "nothing" or "nonsense," is made in several variations. Some recipes include rum or brandy and are often served with stewed plums or other fruit.*

---

2 tablespoons raisins

¼ cup brandy or rum

2 eggs, separated

1 tablespoon granulated sugar

½ cup all-purpose flour

Pinch of salt

1 cup milk

Unsalted butter

In a small bowl soak raisins in brandy until soft. In a large bowl beat egg yolks and sugar until light and creamy. Sift in flour and salt alternately with milk. Mix until smooth. Add drained raisins. In a large bowl beat egg whites until stiff enough to form soft peaks. Fold into the batter to combine well but do not over-fold.

In an 8-inch heavy skillet or omelet pan heat 1 tablespoon of butter over medium heat. Pour in half the batter; cook 4 or 5 minutes, until golden and puffed. Invert onto a warm plate. Butter pan again; return pancake to pan to cook uncooked side until golden and done. With two forks cut into shreds and remove to a warm pan. Heat more butter and cook remaining batter the same way. Serve at once sprinkled with confection's sugar.

Swiss Cherry Soufflé

This recipe is for a typical Swiss fruit soufflé that can be enjoyed for a luncheon or dinner dessert.

¾ cup unsalted butter

1 cup granulated sugar

4 eggs, separated

1 teaspoon grated lemon peel

2 cups ground filberts (hazelnuts)

1 cup graham-cracker crumbs

1 cup heavy cream

1 can (1 pound) pitted red sour cherries, drained

Whipped cream

Preheat the oven to 325 degrees.

In a large bowl cream the butter and sugar. Add egg yolks; beat until light and fluffy. Add lemon rind, nuts, cracker crumbs, and cream. Let stand 10 minutes. Add cherries; mix well. In another large bowl beat egg whites until stiff peaks form Fold into cherry mixture. Pour into a buttered 2½-quart soufflé dish. Bake about 40 minutes. Serve with whipped cream.

Sweet Omelets

The range of sweet omelets is wide. You can make a basic omelet and fill it with orange marmalade or berry preserves before folding, then sprinkle it with rum and ignite. You can also fill omelets with sweetened strawberries, sprinkle it with kirsch and ignite it; or, fill it apples flambéed with brandy, sprinkle with sugar, and glaze it under a hot broiler.

---

3 eggs, separated

2 teaspoons granulated sugar

Pinch salt

2 teaspoons unsalted butter

Confectioners' sugar

In a medium bowl combine egg yolks, sugar, salt, and 1 teaspoon water. Beat until light and creamy. In a large bowl beat egg whites until stiff but not dry. Fold into egg yolk mixture.

In an omelet pan or medium skillet melt butter over medium-high heat. Add egg mixture, spreading evenly with a spatula. Cook without stirring until edges are light brown. Run a knife around the edges to loosen. Fold the omelet in half; turn out onto a warm plate. Sprinkle the top with confectioners' sugar.

Sweet Omelet with Fruit Sauce

6 servings

---

2 cups fruit purée

2 tablespoons cornstarch

2 tablespoons light rum

6 eggs

Pinch of salt

3 tablespoons granulated sugar

2 teaspoons grated lemon or orange peel

¼ cup cold water

Confectioners' sugar

Put fruit purée in a medium saucepan. Mix cornstarch with a little cold water; blend well. Add to fruit. Cook, stirring, over medium-low heat until mixture thickens a little. Stir in rum; keep warm.

Break the eggs into a large bowl. Beat to blend well. Add salt, sugar, lemon peel, and the water. Beat until smooth and creamy. Pour into a buttered omelet pan or medium skillet. Cook over medium-high heat until mixture is set. Sprinkle with confectioners' sugar. With a spatula remove omelet to a warm platter. Fold over from the two sides toward the middle. Serve at once with the warm fruit sauce.

Swiss Bircher Muesli

This traditional Swiss dish, served for breakfast or supper and sometimes as a dessert in Alpine inns, is composed of raw oats, milk, and fruits. It was created by Dr. Max Bircher-Bennera at his famous clinic in Zurich. He advocated a healthful diet based on fresh fruits, nuts, cereals, and raw and cooked vegetables. Whimsically called musli, *"little mousse," it can be made with varieties of flavors and variations.*

2 cups rolled old-fashioned oats

¼ cup oat bran

1¼ cups low-fat milk, cold

1 large red apple, unpeeled, cored, and finely chopped

2 teaspoons fresh lemon juice

½ cup currants or raisins

½ cup chopped walnuts

¼ cup packed dark brown sugar

In a medium bowl combine the oats and oat bran. Add milk. Let stand at room temperature for 50 minutes. Add apple and lemon juice; mix well. Stir in currants, walnuts, and sugar. Mix well. Refrigerate 1 hour before serving.

Caramel Custard

This popular Alpine dessert, also known as creme caramel in French, is a custard baked in a caramel-lined mold or individual custard cups.

¾ cup plus
  3 tablespoons
  granulated sugar
2 cups milk
4 eggs
½ teaspoon orange or
  vanilla extract

Preheat the oven to 375 degrees.

Combine ¾ cup of the sugar and 2 teaspoons water in a heavy skillet over medium-high heat. When the sugar begins to melt, stir, shaking the pan a little. Leave over the heat until the mixture becomes a deep golden syrup. Pour at once into 6 (5-ounce) custard cups.

In a small saucepan scald the milk over medium-high heat. In a medium bowl combine the eggs, remaining 3 tablespoons sugar, and the extract. Pour in the hot milk; beat to blend well. Pour over the caramelized mixture, dividing evenly. Place custard cups in a pan of hot water. Bake about 1 hour, until a knife inserted into center comes out clean. Remove from the oven and from the hot water. Cool. Invert onto a large plate or platter and serve.

Austrian Linzer Torte

This attractive lattice-top cake is one of the most popular of all the great Austrian pastries. It is handsomely displayed in konditorei *(pastry shops) and also prepared in the home for dessert or to serve with afternoon tea.*

¾ cup (1½ sticks) unsalted butter, softened

¾ cup granulated sugar

2 egg yolks

1½ cups finely ground hazelnuts or almonds

2 teaspoons grated lemon peel

1½ cups all-purpose flour

½ teaspoon ground cinnamon

⅛ teaspoon ground cloves

1 cup raspberry or strawberry preserves

Confectioners' sugar

In a large bowl cream the butter and granulated sugar, beating until light and fluffy. Add egg yolks; mix to blend well. Stir in nuts and lemon rind. Into a medium bowl sift the flour, cinnamon, and cloves. Stir a little at a time into the creamed mixture. Mix well. Refrigerate, covered, for 1 hour.

Preheat oven to 375 degrees. Grease a 9-inch springform pan. Spoon three quarters of the mixture into the prepared pan with a removable bottom, spreading evenly. Spoon preserves over the top. Roll out the remaining dough and cut into 8 strips, each about ⅓ inch wide and of varying lengths. Arrange strips of dough over preserves to make a lattice. Bake until crust is golden and tender, about 50 minutes. Cool on a wire rack. Remove from the pan. Dust top with confectioners' sugar. To serve, cut into wedges.

Walnut Cake

In Slovenia a plain or nut-flavored cake is covered with a thick syrup.
This one is made with walnuts.

½ cup (1 stick) unsalted butter

2½ cups granulated sugar

2 eggs, lightly beaten

2 cups sifted all-purpose flour

1 teaspoon baking powder

1 teaspoon baking soda

½ teaspoon ground cinnamon

⅔ cup sour milk

1 cup chopped walnuts

Grated peel of I lemon

Preheat the oven to 350 degrees. Grease a 13x9x7-inch baking pan.

In a large bowl cream the butter. Add 1 cup of the sugar and the eggs; blend well. In a medium bowl mix the flour, baking powder, baking soda, and cinnamon. Add to the sugar mixture alternately with the sour milk. Mix well. Stir in walnuts and lemon rind. Mix to combine thoroughly. Turn into prepared pan. Bake about 45 minutes, until a tester inserted into center comes out clean.

Meanwhile, make a thick syrup by boiling together the remaining 1½ cups sugar and the 1 cup water for 15 minutes. Pour over the cake while it is still warm. Turn off oven and return the cake to the oven for 5 minutes. Cut into diamond shapes. Serve warm or at room temperature.

Strawberries in Wine

In the Alpine countries, excellent desserts are made with a large variety of fresh fruits. Often berries are flavored with liqueur or wine to make a simple dessert, superb for a summer luncheon or dinner.

---

1 quart fresh
   strawberries, hulled

¼ cup granulated
   sugar

½ cup dry white wine

In a bowl or serving dish sprinkle strawberries with sugar. Pour wine over them. Refrigerate, covered, until chilled, 2 to 3 hours.

Italian Stuffed Peaches

6 servings

The delectable, golden peach is one of the favorite fruits in the Italian Alps, where it is used to make compotes, tarts, and this pleasing dessert.

---

6 large peaches

¼ cup blanched almonds

¼ cup crumbled almond macaroons

3 tablespoons granulated sugar

1 teaspoon grated lemon or orange peel

3 tablespoons unsalted butter, melted

Preheat the oven to 350 degrees. Grease a baking dish large enough to hold all the peaches.

Wash and peel peaches. Cut into halves; remove stones and a little pulp around them. Combine almonds, macaroons, sugar, and peel. Spoon into peach cavities.

Arrange in the prepared dish. Sprinkle with the melted butter. Bake 30 minutes.

Poached Pears

In the French Alps these chilled poached pears topped with pureed raspberries and whipped cream is a favorite dinner or late supper dessert.

---

12 firm slightly underripe pears

Juice of 2 lemons

2 cups granulated sugar

2 cups water

2 teaspoons vanilla

2 packages (10 or 12 ounces each) frozen raspberries, partially thawed

2 tablespoons kirsch or other liqueur

Whipped cream

Peel and halve pears. Scoop out cores; cut out stems. Rub the pears with a little lemon juice to prevent darkening. In a medium saucepan combine sugar, water, remaining lemon juice, and vanilla over medium-high heat. Bring to a boil. Cook briskly 5 minutes. Add pears. Reduce heat to medium-low. Simmer, covered, about 10 minutes, or until tender. Remove pears to a serving dish. Reduce syrup over high heat until tender. Pour over pears. Chill.

Meanwhile, process raspberries in a blender or food processor. Add kirsch or liqueur. Serve chilled pears topped with the berry purée and whipped cream.

Italian Cheese and Fruit

A typical Italian dessert is cheese and fruit. Place a large bowl of fresh fruit (plums, pears, apples, oranges, apricots, figs, grapes) on the table. For a choice of cheeses, offer Gorgonzola, Bel Paese, or stracchino on a board or platter.

For each person have a small plate, knife and fork.

Drinks and Wines

It is always a pleasure to enjoy local Alpine beer or wine with a midday or evening meal and to pause any time in between for a favorite libation. Particularly inviting are *kellers, weinstubse, trattorias,* cafés or any gathering place possessing an atmosphere of good cheer; they are known for good drinks, fine food, and sometimes entertainment.

In the realm of Alpine dining, drinks and wines are of considerable importance, and are served at festivals, social events, family celebrations, and particularly when relaxing after a day spent outdoors, skiing, mountain climbing, or pursuing other pleasures. Each country has its favorite libations, differing somewhat from France and Italy to Germany and Slovenia, sometimes imparting nourishment and conviviality. Sharing a cup of cheer is an accepted way of life wherever you are in the Alps. .

In Alpine countries people also enjoy refreshing beverages made with fruit juices, including soft and hard ciders, sparkling and mineral waters, as well as cold and hot teas, coffees, and chocolate drinks. The Swiss, in particular, are truly devotees of chocolate and beverages made with it. Mountaineers carry chocolate with them and hot chocolate is enjoyed throughout the day and night, especially for breakfast and in mid-afternoon. It's the perfect cold-weather beverage. Austrians love their ubiquitous coffeehouses where it is customary to sit, converse, or relax with a cup or two of coffee, served with an appealing variety with breads or pastries.

Drinks classified as spirits, distilled from fruit, known as fruit brandies or eaux-de-vie, "waters of life," are also popular in most of the Alpine nations. *Kirschwasser,* or *kirsch,* as it is most commonly called, is a favorite. It is a fragrant, crystal-clear potent drink with an exquisite flavor made from cherries. In France, Switzerland, and Germany it is enjoyed at the end of a meal, as a digestive. It also goes well with fruit, and is a superb flavoring for desserts and sweet sauces. Italians favor a clear aromatic strong liquor called grappa, made by fermenting and distilling grape pulps left after wine-making. Grappas are always served at room temperature, never chilled. In France marc is a similar drink. In Slovenia, a strong brandy or eau-de-vie called zganje is distilled from several fruits but most commonly plums. The finest brandy, pleterska hruska, is made from pears.

Austrians and Germans relish the custom of pausing in mid-morning for a second, or "fork" breakfast, of sausages, goulash, or some other warming fare, with a glass or two of spirits. Once it was a substantial meal at about 11 A.M. preceded by schnapps, a common term for strong spirits but in particular a clear, potent drink distilled from rye that is commonly tossed back with a beer chaser. Now one generally partakes of a hearty soup or ham and bread with a beer. One can also indulge in a "hangover repast," herring of some kind with sour cream, or a hot soup or stew, with spirits.

Beer

Beer has long been the most common drink in Alpine regions where grapes do not flourish. Over the years the amber brew became very important in everyday life, folklore, and culture and a great deal has been written in literature about beer. Quite naturally the popular beverage was introduced into the local cookery and a number of interesting beer dishes can be found in the various Alpine cuisines.

Germany has for generations been preeminent in brewing and drinking beer where it's the national drink. While nearly every town gives its name to the beer that is brewed there, Bavaria is particularly associated with the drink and has an inordinate fondness for favorite brews. The art of brewing beer is part of Bavaria's heritage and enjoys a high standing. Once brew houses were among the most important buildings and brewing was the most flourishing trade. One old account of Bavarian beers stated that the countless varieties there include black beer, white beer, brown beer, thin beer, strong beer, double beer, and bitter beer.

Munich, the Bavarian capital on the Isar River, has a wealth of famous sights, from theaters and concert halls to churches and museums, including one devoted to beer, as well as countless beer halls and gardens. Since 1591 the enormous Hofbräuhaus, a lively beer hall known for rollicking merriment, has been pouring the drink and now the beer is so famous that it even comes in seasonal varieties. The dark, strong, sweet Bock is brewed in winter and consumed in spring. A light, lager-type beer, Pilsner, and other light-bodied beers such as Weissbier (wheat beer), light in color and usually accompanied by a slice of lemon, are summer favorites. Marzenbier, a special kind of strong beer, is a popular autumn drink but is also drunk in spring.

Drinking beer has long been an important aspect of the city's entertainment scene. Although there are other local festivals important to the Bavarian culture, Munich's Octoberfest is certainly a party one is likely to remember. It's the beer festival supreme. Thousands of enthusiastic beer-drinkers have lived it up every autumn since 1810 to celebrate the city's famous beers. Here the spirit of Gemütlichkeit reigns with oompah bands playing Bavarian folk music, parades, and rides.

Among the unique ranges of beer consumed in enormous quantities from large earthenware and glass mugs are Export (light and dark), Rauchbier (smoked), Kellerbier (a fruity, malty wheat beer), Dunkels (a dark, strong one brewed specially for Lent), or Radler, a fizzy mixture of lemonade and beer.

There is, of course, a large assortment of edibles, from pretzels and radishes to spit-roasted fish, grilled chicken, herring salads, smoked ham, sauerkraut, dumplings, and copious quantities of sausages, especially Weisswurst, eaten with mustard and rolls, and links of bratwurst.

Wines

Here are descriptions of a few of the better known Alpine wines.

French Wines

Savoy, or Savoie, in the foothills of the French Alps tucked in between Switzerland, Italy, and the French provinces of La Bresse and Dauphine, is the most mountainous region of France and vineyards prosper in the rugged valleys. From this land of fresh Alpine air and clear lakes come delightful white and sparkling wines that have finish and style but do not travel well so they are best enjoyed in the locales where they come from. The whites are delicate and full of body. The best known is Crépy, a light dry wine with a hint of violet from the French shores of Lake Geneva, made primarily from the Chasselas grape. Seyssel, an interesting pale, fresh, light wine, is produced around the town of the same name near the headwaters of the Rhone River. Here there are some fresh, fragrant white wines made from the Roussette or Roussanne grape which, according to local legend, was brought to the area from Cyprus in the middle of the fifteenth century. This same grape is also used to make Seyssel Mousseux, an excellent sparkling wine.

Swiss Wines

Switzerland produces many excellent wines from vineyards along its sunny lake shores to those with terraces at over 3,600 feet near the Matterhorn. They are as varied as the climates and soils in which they flourish. For the most part, however, the viticulture areas follow the four national languages: Swiss-German and Romansch in the East, French in the West, and Italian in the South.

All Swiss wine names are geographic and carry the name of a specific region, canton, local town, or parish. More than half of all Swiss wine is white, made from the Chasselas grape that produces a fresh, lively wine. It has a natural sparkle or crispness that distinguishes it from the wines of nearby vineyards in other countries.

In the east, the Thurgau, Schaffhausen, and Lake Constance areas, plus the Alpine valley of the Rhine, the red, white, and rosé wines are light and subtle. Since many of the best Swiss wines never even leave where they are made, the only way to enjoy their wonderfully diverse tastes is to travel to the places or origin. It's always a pleasure to enjoy a good local wine with the delicious food.

Liechtenstein Wines

The making of wine is very important in Liechtenstein with nearly the entire grape harvest made into wines and sold in the principality. Thanks to favorable natural conditions, ideal southwest-oriented hillside locations with calcareous soil, and adequate sunshine, grapes can easily come to full ripeness. Wine quality is comparable to that of nearby Swiss growing areas. Besides Pinot Gris, Chardonnay, Gewuztraminer, and Zweigelt, mainly Pinot Noir and Riesling-x-Sylvaner are cultivated and processed into wines.

Wine names are usually geographic with that of the local town or parish added. Today the making of wine is often in the hands of small owners in areas around the various communities. Visitors to the principality can enjoy wine tastings at several restaurants and inns as well as at the princely vineyards.

Italian Wines

Some of Italy's finest wines are produced in the small mountain villages of Piedmont. Of particular fame are two red wines famous around the world. Barolo, often called the best red in Italy, full-bodied, deep-colored with a high alcohol content, is made from the great nebbiolo grape in a small hilly district of which the town of Barola is the center. Barbaresco, strong, slow-maturing, and justly celebrated, is made from the same grape in two townships, Barbaresco and Nieve. While it develops completeness at an early age and is light, it is a wine of true distinction.

Another well-known wine is the rather sweet, slightly flowery, sparkling white Asti Spumante. It is excellent at the end of a meal with dessert and fruit. Asti, an important wine town, is also a major center of the trade for vermouth, a fortified white wine with various flavorings and a favorite Italian aperitif.

Lombardy also produces wines in three districts. Interesting and unusual red wines from Valtellina are produced from grapes grown at great heights on terraced vineyards near the Swiss border. There are also some agreeable red and white wines from the Italian Tirolian district.

German Wines

In Bavaria, grape-growing goes back to Roman times, although as a result of the favorable climate, it now extends along the River Main in Franconia, and to a small but attractive area located on Lake Constance, around Lindau, Wasserburg, and Nonnenhorn. Like beer, Bavaria's wines from Franconia enjoy a great reputation and are bottled in a distinctive bulbous bottle called a Bocksbeutel. The whites, Silvaner and Muller-Thurgau, and a rare red, Schqarzriegling, are highly rated.

Austrian Wines

By tradition Austria is a wine-drinking country and vineyards once covered a great many acres. Now viticulture is confined to four main districts in the east. These include Burgenland or Bergland, along the border with Hungary; Styria in the southeast; lower Austria; and area around Vienna.

Almost all of the Austrian wines are white, refreshing, fairly dry, fruity, and low in alcohol with a good bouquet. Many of them carry names from a variety of grapes, such as Riesling, Gewurztraminer, Sylvaner, Muller-Thurgau, plus such local favorites as Veltliner and Rotgipfler.

Most visitors to Austria are likely to enjoy the young, fresh white wines at typical drinking places called *heurigen* that, from spring to early fall, consist of a garden setting with long wooden tables and benches. Another aspect of the Austrian wine experience is the *keller*, in essence is a rustic tavern blended with the ambiance of a wine cellar.

Slovenian Wines

Wine has a long history in Slovenia where it flourished under the Romans and many of their architectural remains are decorated with grape motifs. Today the country's wine production and methods of viticulture are typically Austrian due to the proximity of the Adriatic Sea on the west and the Danube plain to the east, moderating the Alpine climate and providing mild winters and temperate summers.

Slovenia has three primary wine-growing regions: the Adriatic shore, the basin of the River Drava, and the basin of the River Sava. The most important is the basin of the Drava with the famous Ljutomer, a white table wine sometimes called Lutomer. Most of the wines are identified by the regional wine.

The best known wine of the River Sava is the pink Cvicek, a light fresh rose, and most important of the Adriatic wines is the red Kraski Teran from the northern part of Istria. It has an ancient reputation for having curative powers, perhaps because of its richness in iron and tannin.

Bibliography

Beer, Gretel. *Exploring Rural Austria*. Chicago: Passport Books, 1990.

Fitzgibbon, Theodora. *The Food of the Western World*. New York: Quadrangle, 1976.

Fodor, Eugene. *Fodor's Guide to Europe*. The Hague: Morton & Co., 1965.

Fodor's 2002 Switzerland. New York: Fodor Travel Publications, 2002.

Fleming, Fergus. *Killing Dragons: The Conquest of the Alps*. New York: Atlantic Monthly Press, 2000.

Green, Vivian H. *The Swiss Alps*. London, B.T. Batsford Ltd., 1961.

Maeder, Herbert. *The Mountains of Switzerland*. New York: Walker and Company, 1967.

Nelson, Kay Shaw Nelson. *The Best of Western European Cooking*. New York: John Day, 1976.

The Eastern European Cookbook. Chicago: Henry Regnery, 1973.

Ogrizek, Dore and J.G. Rufenacht. *Switzerland*. New York: McGraw Hill, l949.

Reifsnyder, William E. and Marylou. *Adventuring in the Alps*. San Francisco: Sierra Club Books, 1986.

Recipe Index

Subject Index

Grosslockner, 13
Gstaad, 11
Gulf of Genoa, 9

Hannibal, 9
Hemingway, Ernest, 15, 78
Hitler, Adolph, 14
Hohenschwangau, 7
Hungary, 15

Innsbruck, 13, 81, 128
Inn River, 7, 13, 128
Interlaken, 11, 28
Italy, 5, 9, 13, 15, 179, 182

Julian Alps, 9, 15
Jungfrau, 11

Karavanke range, 13, 15
Kitzbuhel, 13, 21
Klosters, 11
Kobarid, 15, 78
Kranjska Gora, 15, 117
Kreuzeck, 14

La Bresse, 182
Lake
   Constance, 14, 182
   Geneva, 11, 182
   Konigsee, 14
   Leman, 71
Liechtenstein, 9, 12, 25, 48, 136, 182
Lindau, 14
Linderhof, 7
Lombardy, 137, 147, 148, 183
Ljubljana, 15
Ludwig II, King, 7

Malhun, 12
Marmolata, 12
Matterhorn, 11, 182
Mediterranean Sea, 9, 10
Megeve, 10
Milan, Italy, 5, 96, 147
Mittenwald, 157
Mont
   Aiguille, 10
   Blanc, 6, 9, 10, 27, 160
   Dom, 74
   Katrin, 13
   Rosa, 11
   Triglav, 15, 24
   Watzmann, 14
Monte Bondone, 12
Munich, 14, 181

Nelson, Rae, 6
Neuschwanstein, 103
Nice, 10
Nuremberg, 103

Obergurgl, 7, 13
Obersalzberg, 14
Octoberfest, 14, 181
Ortles-Cenedale, 12

Parco dello Stelvio, 12
Pass of Comporosso, 15
Piedmont, 31, 70, 125, 153
Piran, 15, 87
Podravje, 15
Po River, 9, 147
Posavje, 15
Predel Pass, 15

Also by Kay Shaw Nelson...

All Along the Rhine
Recipes, Wines and Lore from Germany, France, Switzerland, Austria, Liechtenstein and Holland

This wonderful collection of over 130 recipes spans the range of home cooking, from Appetizers, Soups, Main Courses, and Side Dishes, to Desserts and Beverages. Among the recipes included are traditional favorites and signature dishes from the six countries: Cheese Fondue, Balzers Split Pea-Sausage Stew, Alpine Sauerkraut Soup, Bratwurst in Beer, and Pears in Red Wine.

Each chapter covers the culinary history and winemaking tradition of a different Rhine country. The literary excerpts, legends and lore throughout the book will enchant the reader-chef on this culinary cruise down one of the world's most famous rivers.

230 PAGES • 5½ X 8½ • B/W PHOTOS • 0-7818-0830-8 • $24.95HC • (89)
$14.95PB • (444)

The Scottish-Irish Pub & Hearth Cookbook

From hearty, wholesome recipes for family dinners, to more sophisticated and exotic dishes for entertaining with flair, this book is the perfect source for dining the Celtic way! In this collection of 170 recipes of the best of Scottish and Irish pub fare and home cooking, you'll find old classics like Corn Beef `N Cabbage, Cock-A-Leekie, Avalon Apple Pie, and Fish and Chips, and new recipes as well: Tobermory Smoked Salmon Pâté, Raisin Walnut Porridge, and Skibbereen Scallop-Mushroom Pie. Each chapter begins with entertaining stories, legends, and lore about Celtic peoples, traditions, customs, and history.

260 PAGES • 5½ X 8½ • B/W PHOTOS/ILLUSTRATIONS • 0-7818-0741-7 • $24.95HC • (164)

Cuisines of the Caucasus Mountains
Recipes, Drinks and Lore from Armenia, Azerbaijan, Georgia, and Russia

With healthful and delectable ingredients like pomegranates, saffron, rose water, honey, olive oil, yogurt, onions, garlic, fresh and dried fruits, and a variety of nuts, these 184 authentic recipes provide many delicious options. The literary excerpts, legends, and lore sprinkled throughout the book will also enchant the reader-chef on his culinary journey to one of the world's most famous mountain ranges.

269 PAGES • 6 X 9 • B/W PHOTOS/ILLUSTRATIONS • 0-7818-0928-2 • $24.95HC • (37)

Other cookbooks of interest from Hippocrene ...

All Along the Danube, Expanded Edition

Recipes from Germany, Austria, Czechoslovakia, Yugoslavia, Hungary, Romania, and Bulgaria
Marina Polvay

Now updated with a section on classic Central European wines!

For novices and gourmets, this unique cookbook offers a tempting variety of more than 300 Central European recipes from the shores of the Danube River, bringing Old World flavor to today's dishes.

357 PAGES • 5½ X 8½ • B/W PHOTOS/ILLUSTRATIONS • 0-7818-0806-5 • $14.95PB • (479)

Best of Austrian Cuisine

Elisabeth Mayer-Browne

Nearly 200 recipes from Austria's rich cuisine: roasted meats in cream sauces, hearty soups and stews, tasty dumplings, and of course, the pastries and cakes that remain Vienna's trademark.

224 PAGES • 5 X 8½ • 0-7818-0526-0 • $11.95PB •(633)

The Swiss Cookbook

Nika Standen Hazelton

Drawing from her long experience of and affection for Switzerland, Nika Hazelton explains the basic elements of Swiss cooking as it is practiced in Swiss homes. Her "lessons" include directions for "au bleu" fish cookery, for making superb dumplings or Swiss pasta, for fondue in all its variations, and for roasting veal in the Swiss manner. The book's 250 recipes, gathered over many years from peasants, housewives, and chefs through history, cover the range of home cooking, from appetizers to desserts, all adapted for the American kitchen.

236 PAGES • 5½ X 8½ • 0-7818-0587-2 • $11.95PB • (726)

The Art of Dutch Cooking
C. Countess van Limburg Stirum

This attractive volume offers a complete cross section of Dutch home cooking, adapted to American kitchens. A whole chapter is devoted to the Dutch Christmas, with recipes for the cookies and candies that are a traditional part of the festivities. There are also chapters on potatoes (a national favorite), on party beverages—including several superb champagne punches—and on Indonesian dishes from the Dutch East Indies. Many of the 200 recipes can be wholly or partially prepared beforehand.

192 PAGES • 5½ X 8¼ • 0-7818-0582-1 • $11.95PB • (683)

Taste of Romania, Expanded Edition
Nicolae Klepper

Now updated with a chapter of Romanian-Jewish Recipes!

"A brilliant cultural and culinary history … a collection of recipes to be treasured, tested and enjoyed." —George Lang, owner of Café des Artiste

" … dishes like creamy cauliflower soup, sour cream-enriched *mamaliga* (the Romanian polenta), lamb stewed in sauerkraut juice and scallions, and *mititei* (exactly like the ones I tasted so long ago in Bucharest) are simple and appealing . . . Klepper paints a pretty picture of his native country's culinary possibilities." —Colman Andrews, *Saveur* magazine

A real taste of both Old World and modern Romanian culture. More than 140 recipes, including the specialty dishes of Romania's top chefs, are intermingled with fables, poetry, photos and illustrations in this comprehensive and well-organized guide to Romanian cuisine.

335 PAGES • 6 X 9 • B/W PHOTOS/ILLUSTRATIONS • 0-7818-0766-2 • $24.95HC • (462)

The Art of Hungarian Cooking, Revised Edition
Paula Pogany Bennett and Velma R. Clark

Now updated with a concise guide to Hungarian wines!

Whether you crave Chicken Paprika or Apple Strudel, these 222 authentic Hungarian recipes include a vast array of national favorites, from appetizers through desserts.

225 PAGES •5½ X 8½ • B/W DRAWINGS • 0-7818-0586-4 • $11.95PB • (686)

Hungarian Cookbook
Old World Recipes for New World Cooks
Yolanda Nagy Fintor

These Old World recipes were brought to America by the author's grandparents, but they have been updated to accommodate the modern lifestyle. Hungarian cuisine is known for generous amounts of paprika, sour cream, bacon and garlic in famous dishes like Chicken Paprika and Hungarian Goulash. This collection includes these classics, and spans the range of home cooking with recipes for Bean with Sausage Soup, Stuffed Breast of Veal, Hungarian Creamed Spinach, and a host of tempting desserts like Walnut Torte, and Dilled Cottage Cheese Cake.

This is more than just a collection of 125 enticing Hungarian recipes. Eight chapters also describe the seasonal and ceremonial holidays that Hungarian-Americans celebrate today with special foods: fall grape festivals; Christmas, New Year's and Easter; summer cookouts; weddings and baptisms. The book also includes culinary tips, a glossary of terms and explanations about the Hungarian language.

190 PAGES • 5½ X 8¼ • $24.95HC • 0-7818-0828-6 • (47)

The Best of Polish Cooking, Expanded Edition
Karen West

Now updated with a new chapter on Light Polish Fare!

"Ethnic cuisine at its best."—*The Midwest Book Review*

First published in 1983, this classic resource for Polish cuisine has been a favorite with home chefs for many years. The new edition includes a chapter on Light Polish Fare with ingenious tips for reducing fat, calories and cholesterol, without compromising the flavor of fine Polish cuisine. Fragrant herbal rubs and vinegars add panache without calories. Alternatives and conversion tables for butter, sour cream and milk will help readers lighten other recipes as well.

In an easy-to-use menu format, the author arranges complementary and harmonious foods together—all organized in seasonal cycles. Inside are recipes for Braised Spring Lamb with Cabbage, Frosty Artichoke Salad, Apple Raisin Cake, and Hunter's Stew. The new Light Polish Fare chapter includes low-fat recipes for treats like Roasted Garlic and Mushroom Soup and Twelve-Fruit Brandied Compote.

248 PAGES • 5½ X 8¼ • $9.95PB • 0-7818-0826-X • (274)

The Best of Czech Cooking, Expanded Edition
Peter Trnka

Now expanded with three new chapters on Pork, Mushrooms, and Drinks, this popular Hippocrene cookbook is better than ever. Czech cuisine emphasizes delicious soups, salads, dumplings, hearty meat dishes, vegetables and desserts, with recipes that rely on the subtle flavors of fresh ingredients. This new edition includes *Vepro-knedlo-zelo*, a classic dish of pork, cabbage and dumplings; an informative chapter about gathering, storing and using wild mushrooms; and a section on aperitifs, wine and beers, including the world-famous Czech Pilsner Urquell beer.
300 PAGES • 5½ X 8¼ • 0-7818-0805-7 • $24.95HC • (456)

The Best of Slovak Cooking
Sylvia & John Lorinc

This cookbook features more than 100 easy-to-follow Slovak recipes. Along with creative preparation of certain staples such as potatoes, cabbage and noodles, Slovak cuisine is also noted for its pastries, rich butter and cream dishes, and pork specialties. Among the chapters included are: Soups, Vegetables & Side Dishes, Main Dishes, and Desserts & Breads. All recipes are adapted for the North American kitchen.
138 PAGES • 5½ X 8¼ • 0-7818-0765-4 • $22.50HC • (543)

Art Of Lithuanian Cooking
Maria Gieysztor de Gorgey

With more than 150 recipes, this cookbook is a collection of traditional hearty Lithuanian favorites including Fresh Cucumber Soup, Lithuanian Meat Pockets, Hunter's Stew, Potato Zeppelins, and delicacies like Homemade Honey Liqueur and Easter Gypsy Cake.
178 PAGES • 5½ X 8½ • 0-7818-0610-0 • $22.50HC • (722)

Prices subject to change without prior notice. To purchase HIPPOCRENE
BOOKS contact your local bookstore, call (718) 454-2366, or write to:
HIPPOCRENE BOOKS, 171 Madison Avenue, New York, NY 10016.
Please enclose check or money order, adding $5.00 shipping (UPS) for the first book,
and $.50 for each additional book.